Conscious Endeavors:

Essays on Business, Society and the Journey to Sustainability

CONSCIOUS ENDEAVORS: ESSAYS ON BUSINESS, SOCIETY AND THE JOURNEY TO SUSTAINABILITY.

First published 2009 by Scriptorium/Palimpsest Press, an imprint of Green Frigate Books

FIRST EDITION

ISBN-10: 139780971X
ISBN-13: 9781397809711

Printing this book on recycled stock has saved:
132 trees, 56,672 gallons of water, 22,796 kwh electricity, 6,244 lbs solid waste and 12,276 greenhouse gasses

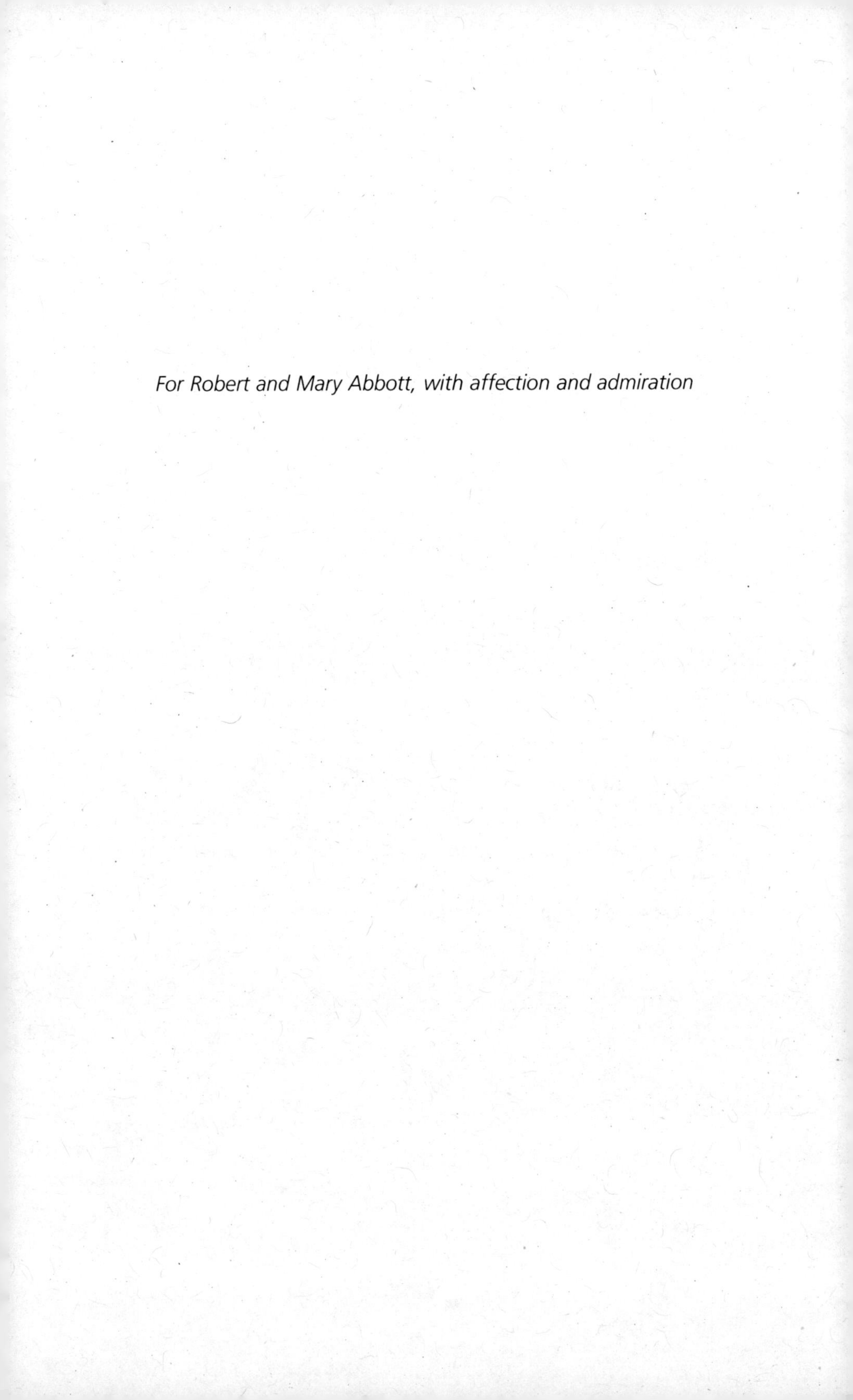

For Robert and Mary Abbott, with affection and admiration

I know of no more encouraging fact than the unquestionable ability of man to elevate his life by conscious endeavor. It is something to be able to paint a particular picture, or to carve a statue, and so to make a few objects beautiful; but it is far more glorious to carve and paint the very atmosphere and medium through which we look...To affect the quality of the day, that is the highest of arts.

—Henry David Thoreau

Business today consists in persuading crowds

—T.S. Eliot

Most businesses are behaving as if people were still scarce and nature still abundant – the conditions that helped to fuel the first Industrial Revolution. The logic of economizing on the scarcest resource because it limits progress remains correct. But the pattern of scarcity is shifting. Now people aren't scarce, but nature is.

—Paul Hawken

Do or do not. There is no try.

—Yoda, Jedi Master

Contents

Preface: A Word about this Book and its Structure

I have spent more than half my life studying businesses around the world, and advising many of those businesses on how to create wealth through a deep integration of sustainability with core business strategy. I have also had the privilege to teach at a variety of universities in North America and abroad, and to support the work of several non-governmental organizations (NGOs) working at the nexus of business, government and society. Collectively, these experiences have shaped my thinking on the responsibility of business to society, and spurred the writing of many of the essays and speeches that make up this collection.

Quite apart from my academic and professional interest, I come by my love of the land honestly; I grew up in a hunting, fishing and camping family where reverence for the natural world was instilled at an early age – and nurtured thereafter. Much of this book was written in the shadow of a mountain, or near the edge of the sea. I make my living as a consultant, writer and speaker – work that finds me in cities much of the time, but I am at my best, most fully realized self in nature. It is that spirit that hopefully tempers and adds nuance to this collection – it is a book about business, but it is also something of a personal declaration of sustainability and the questions I think we need to answer if we are to forge a new generation of businesses, and the people who work in them, that is sustainable.

This book consists of four sections:

Origins

Every journey has a beginning. In this first section I turn over some stones that reveal stories and ideas about business, society and the journey to sustainability that have informed the work I have done, and might yet do.

Homage

We all stand on the shoulders of the giants who came before us. Here, I profile eight people whose words and example inspire me, and whose legacy I try to honor. Too often we forget our history and the efforts of those who came before us. The work of these authors and scholars is worth discovering anew because it is, firstly, dazzlingly well written. It also represents something of an environmental or sustainability canon with which students, practitioners and interested readers should become familiar. It inspired me, and inspires me still; it might do likewise for readers who are introduced to it, however briefly, in these pages. Most important, many of the perspectives and, dare I say it, *answers* that we need to shift business and society onto a more sustainable trajectory can be found here.

Reflection

The landscape architect, Garrett Eckbo, in his seminal text, *Landscape for Living* (1950), deftly used a remark from Christopher Cauldwell to anchor his argument. He said, in part, "we must know to be able to do, but we must feel to know what to do." This requires reflection. In this section, I reflect on what I have observed and learned of human – environmental interactions and the particular role of business as an agent of change in the natural, social and economic environments. The pieces in this section are my attempt to make sense of it – the better to be able to know what to do.

Renewal

The most important question in any book that hopes to say something about business and society is "where are we going?" In this concluding section, I offer some thoughts on how we might answer this question in ways that allow us to forge a future that is more kind, more just, and more humane – to ourselves and to the planet we call home.

At the beginning of each section I include personal essays that go some distance toward charting my journey to sustainability and explaining my connection to the land and why I do what I do. A coda, following section 4, expands on these essays and here I deliberately use Barry

Lopez' invocation to "lean into the light" as an organizing frame. This is a book about business and society, but our personal experiences, our histories, and most especially our experiences with the land, shape how we think about business and society. The coda explores this idea and in doing so, serves as a capstone for the book as a whole.

There is some repetition of case studies and stories throughout the book. While I have tried to keep this to a minimum, I believe that some messages are sufficiently important that they deserve to be repeated. I also believe that this is a book that a reader can dip into, rather than one that must be read sequentially or in some other kind of "order". By repeating a few core messages or case studies I hope to reach the widest possible audience and demonstrate that we all have the capacity to elevate ourselves through conscious endeavor.

I have included notes at the end of each section that amplify particular ideas and provide additional context or information on a particular point in the text. An index is included to assist the reader in finding key topics quickly, and a web resource guide and bibliography provides guidance on what I consider to be the most important and interesting work on business, society and the journey to sustainability.

—Rob Abbott

Calgary, Alberta & Point Reyes Station, California, 2008

Acknowledgements

To the memory of my late parents, Robert and Mary Abbott, who nurtured my curiosity about the world and kept it stoked through the years with love, support, good questions, and, when necessary, epicurean care packages.

To Robert France, the dearest of friends for twenty-five years, and the most enthusiastic and gifted writer I know. Thank you, Bob; you deserve to see in print how important your friendship has been to me. To Mark Holland and Anita Burke, two friends and colleagues who know what it is to stand in the fire, and who have helped me face, and make, life-changing decisions with a brave heart and a clear head. To Sarah Kerr, for introducing me to the poetry of Dawna Markova, and especially for acting as spirit guide during a pivotal moment in my life. And to Mary Oliver, who knows that wonderful things happen at edges, and who writes like an angel.

To some truly extraordinary clients over the years who have made my personal journey so much more satisfying that it might otherwise have been. In particular, Lorna Seppala, David Balser, Bruce Sampson and Sarah Severn made the good days much better and the bad days a good deal less bad.

I'm grateful to the Mesa Refuge in Point Reyes Station, California, which provided a much-needed retreat for writing – I completed this manuscript at the Refuge, and benefited from conversations with my fellow writers-in-residence, Charlie Cray and Vanessa Huang. I am especially grateful to Charlie for introducing me to the work of Edward Alsworth Ross.

Finally, this entire undertaking would not have been possible without the love and support of my partner, Monica Pohlmann, and stepdaughter, Portia Burton. Namaste.

Introduction

Overheard on Air Canada flight 118 from Calgary to Toronto (June 14, 2006): *"We just throw them away. They're disposable".*

Air Canada flight attendant to passenger describing what is done with the airline's headphones.

Rachel Carson began *Silent Spring,* her 1962 book that has been an intellectual and moral compass in my life, and many others, with an artful play on Robert Frost's poem, The Road Not Taken. In her words:

> We stand now where two roads diverge. But unlike the roads in Robert Frost's familiar poem, they are not equally fair. The road we have long been traveling is deceptively easy; a smooth superhighway on which we progress with great speed, but at its end lays disaster. The other fork of the road - the one "less traveled by" - offers our last, our only chance to reach a destination that assures the preservation of our earth."

While the word "sustainability" was not yet part of the popular lexicon in 1962, I know in my bones that Carson was pointing us in this direction – toward a renewed relationship with the earth and with each other; toward a world in which economic, social, environmental and cultural aspirations are considered not as isolated goals, but as interdependent parts of a single system[i].

Forty-seven years later, we stand tentatively in the doorway of a new century, looking at all that might unfold before us. And there is much discussion and debate about the relationships between environmental protection, economic development, and social welfare. The things that distinguish one company from another and the role, if any, that sustainability might play in this regard is a particularly boisterous discussion. How much we have yet to learn! As George Brandy, Manager of Sustainability Strategies for Interface, put it in a speech echoing Martin Luther King:

> "…the manacles of air toxicity and the chains of global warming still cripple the life of our young children. Our young children live on a lonely island of poverty in the midst of a vast ocean of privatized corporate wealth and socialized public risk.

John Robinson and Caroline Van Bers at the University of British Columbia described our global plight in equally stark terms:

> We are faced with a staggering set of ecological, economic, and social problems, including massive environmental degradation; global economic integration coupled with financial instability, structural unemployment, debt crises, and widening gaps between rich and poor peoples; and a crisis of governance and social problems marked by increased militarism, social and ethnic unrest, and tribalism of various kinds. It is our position that all of these phenomena are connected, and that all are evidence of the growing ecological, economic, and social un-sustainability of business-as-usual patterns of development.

You can see evidence of these problems in virtually every city around the world, and in the hinterland regions that support those cities. My newly adopted home of Calgary, Alberta has been basking in the glow of an economic boom, but it's a boom fueled by fossil fuels, and despite the new wealth being created, there is a disquietingly large number of people living on the streets[ii]. And David Schindler, one of the world's foremost environmental scientists, warns that Alberta, if not Canada, faces a looming water crisis[iii]. Angela Stewart, in a beautiful and thoughtful essay published in the January 22, 2008 edition of *The Globe and Mail*, Canada's national newspaper, honed in on the particular features of the Alberta character and psyche in the face of these challenges:

> We are a wealthy people, most of us, but we do not come from wealthy families. Our parents and grandparents knew

> sweat and failure, farming and fasting, frozen blowing landscapes with the fence down in the far field and the cows roaming loose.
>
> The last generation has paid our admission and we are enjoying the show, not certain we belong but not giving a damn either. We are the roaring Twenties here, but instead of flapper dresses, the Charleston and Model Ts, we've got Lululemon, yoga classes and shiny, clean pickup trucks.
>
> And all the world is watching, it seems, judging us and our snow, our money and our spending, our emissions and admissions.

Most of us, I suspect, can identify with this diagnosis. The specifics may differ, but the underlying message is the same – we have yet to take the other fork of the road. As a society we have yet to commit to living as part of the earth by understanding development as a process to be sustained, not exploited to impractical limits. It is time for all of us to truly honor the legacy of Rachel Carson and begin to live in the world. Or, as James Kunstler has made clear in his trenchant commentaries on American suburbia, begin to dwell in the "hopeful present" and not the "asteroid belt of architectural garbage" that passes for too much of modern America (and a good many other places too). And if it wasn't obvious, this means saying no to "mutilated urbanism," nature "band-aids" that masquerade as ecologically intact green spaces, and the Caesar salad with the 3000-mile supply chain at the local diner – all colorful, and apt markers of our un-sustainability courtesy of Kunstler[iv]. Wendell Berry, an equally potent, if more poetic critic of North American life, puts it this way:

> We face a choice that is starkly simple: we must change or be changed. If we fail to change for the better, then we will be changed for the worse.

The news is not all bad[v]; I believe we're making some progress, but we need to ask if our efforts are transactional rather than transformative. We need to ask if we are doing the best we can within the rules of the game, or whether we are actively working to create a wholly new game. I believe that we need to increasingly make a pledge to resist the routine, the transactional; that we need to resist the tendency to become incredibly good at things that don't necessarily create the future we want – or need.

In 1990, the Swiss industrialist, Stephen Schmidheiny, the founder of the World Business Council for Sustainable Development (WBCSD), predicted that the world was poised for a new industrial revolution based on a more strategic approach to environmental management. As he put it:

> "...it is the most forceful trend in my lifetime. It will reshape business because it will redefine the rules of the game."

On the one hand, I think many of us would agree with those words. But I think we would also agree that the revolution hasn't yet happened, or is in the early stages. I can think of at least two reasons for this. The first speaks to the fact that people are slow to change. There's a well-worn story about a 17th century English sea captain that illustrates this beautifully. In 1601, James Lancaster served lemon juice to the crew on one of four ships he was commanding on a trip to India. Most of the crew on this one ship remained healthy, but on the other three ships, 110 of 278 sailors (40%) died of scurvy by the journey's midpoint. Now, this was important stuff to 17th century seafarers because scurvy claimed more lives than anything else, including warfare. So, you'd think Lancaster's experiment would ignite revolutionary change. Not so. The British Navy didn't stock citrus fruit on its ships until 1795 – nearly 200 years later. Despite the magnitude of the problem, and the availability of a simple solution, people were slow to change. And so it may be for the transition to sustainability. The second reason we haven't seen the full flowering of a new industrial revolution was artfully described by Michael Shellenberger and Ted Nordhaus in their essay, *The Death of Environmentalism*, and subsequent book, *Breakthrough*: "most people wake up in the morning trying to reduce what they have to worry about. Environmentalists wake up trying to increase it". Shellenberger and Nordhaus argue persuasively that the first generation institutional frameworks that evolved to address acid rain, smog and other environmental issues are inadequate to address climate change and other contemporary sustainability challenges. Environmentalism as we know it must "die" so that something new can be born. Society must transcend small-bore environmentalism and interest-group liberalism to create a politics focused as much on uncommon greatness as the common good.

It pains me to say that, however harsh the Schellenberger and Nordhaus critique might first appear, those of us with an interest in sustainability are still largely viewed as little more than latter-day environmentalists or interest group liberals. This is particularly true of our relationship with business. We need to build a bridge to understanding that helps us work to mutual benefit. This requires that the business community think beyond next-quarter financial results, to be sure, but it also requires that we develop a deeper appreciation for how business strategy is created and implemented. The reasons for this are many, but hinge on an important question that lies at the heart of business strategy:

How do organizations form a vision of where they need or want to go?

The answer to this question is vital because it speaks not only to the activities that will be carried out, but also to the culture of the organization – the "way things are done". This latter point is very meaningful for me; it speaks to a fundamental role of management: to see the organization not as it is; but as it can become. *As it can become*. I love that expression and the image of change and opportunity it suggests.

How does a firm decide what it wants to be, what it wants to do? Does it want to shape the evolutionary trajectory of the industry of which it is a part; adapt to opportunities as they present themselves; or reserve the right to play under several possible scenarios by making incremental investments? The answer to this question is important – it will define the particular source(s) of advantage around which the firm builds its strategy[vi]. Every action that is taken, every effort to create value, flows from this decision. As advocates for sustainability, if we can understand, or better still, contribute to the creation of this strategic map, we can more effectively demonstrate where and how sustainability supports broad business strategy. And of course, the reverse is also true; failure to engage business in this way condemns us to working at the margins of the organization and having little influence over its opportunities – to create value for shareholders, but to perhaps do something larger, to create value for society.

How to begin to have this conversation, to begin creating a story that resonates for businesses and the people who work in them? We are, after all, at a defining moment in our history. As Ronald Wright put it in his extraordinary book, *A Short History of Progress:*

> The vessel we are now aboard is not merely the biggest of all time; it is also the only one left. The future of everything we have accomplished since our intelligence evolved will depend on the wisdom of our actions over the next few years. Like all creatures, humans have made their way in the world so far by trial and error; unlike other creatures, we have a presence so colossal that error is a luxury we can no longer afford. The world has grown too small to forgive us any big mistakes.

Today, the enormous gap between the world's wealthiest countries and the remainder of the planet is creating a "resources versus repression" climate that manifests itself in many different and frightening ways. Unless we begin to address this fundamental global problem – which includes issues of economic efficiency, fairness, the scale of the economy relative to the ecosystem, and the dark side of consumerism - we should expect to see more civil unrest, more political dissent and more conflict. Eugene Linden said it well in the paperback edition of his provocative book, *The Future in Plain Sight:*

> The consumer society's images and values invade every corner of the earth, beguiling the young but threatening traditional hierarchies and traditional mores. The more powerful we became and the longer we escaped the terrorist acts that are commonplace elsewhere, the less we worried about offending

> the sensitivities of other cultures as we pursued our global business agenda. In this sense, our very power raised the likelihood of an attack, and our growing sense of invulnerability bred a laxness that greatly raised the probability that an attack would be successful. Few now doubt the destabilizing aspects of religious fanaticism.

Further, the *Millennium Ecosystem Assessment*, the most comprehensive study yet completed of the state of the Earth's natural capital assets, underscored the risk we now face as a global community[vii]. The report noted that human actions are putting such strain on the environment that the ability of the planet's ecosystem to sustain future generations can no longer be taken for granted. Amazing. Hold those words for a moment and think about their meaning; create a picture in your mind of the kind and scale of environmental distress and destruction that makes human life on our planet no longer certain. We are bringing the Earth to its knees, and in doing so we are jeopardizing not only our own lives, but also those of all who might follow us. Viewed in this light, we need to remember our better selves, those features of our character that have allowed us to overcome seemingly intractable obstacles in our past. In a recent roundtable discussion on climate change sponsored by The Sierra Club, Al Gore noted that America did just this in staring down slavery:

> In American politics, there have been soaring moments throughout our history when the truth has swept aside entrenched power. In the darkest hours of our Civil War, Abraham Lincoln said "We must disenthrall ourselves, and then we shall save our country." We need once again to disenthrall ourselves.

Indeed. As someone who advises individuals and organizations on strategy, I'm all-too-familiar with the lament that our world is too complex and fast-paced to understand, much less control. But is that lament too easy, a convenient crutch against the kind of rigorous intellectual and emotional engagement needed to disenthrall us? Have too many of us simply wandered into the organizational forest and lost our collective way? I've given a good deal of thought lately to this question and see a five-point plan to help renew our businesses, our society and ourselves:

(i) Reflect more
(ii) Define a genuine sense of purpose
(iii) Take more risks
(iv) Be more transparent
(v) Think about stakeholder value

Collectively, the ideas embodied in this plan serve as a through line for the essays and speeches in this book.

We all need to reflect more. We need to cultivate a point-of-view about the future that is uniquely our own, and to frame that point-of-view in the context of what is going on around us. Virtually every business claims to do this, but in fact very few pull it off. Why? Because it takes time. Not a huge amount of it – particularly when measured against the costs of framing the business' *raison d'etre* properly – but more than many businesses think they can spare[viii]. Here's a litmus test, if you've ever wondered why your company is doing one thing, and not *doing something else*, you're probably not alone, and your company would likely benefit from framing its work (and communicating same) better. Put another way, what are the opportunity costs associated with a particular program or service? What do you want your legacy to be? Are you and your colleagues genuinely excited about your work? These questions can only be answered after some honest reflection.

With reflection comes the ability to define (or redefine) who you are and why you exist. In a business context, the English management sage, Charles Handy, put it well when he said that the purpose of a business was not to make profits, full stop. Profits were the means to the greater end of doing something more – giving back to the community and having a genuinely positive impact in the world[ix]. So think about your company and ask yourself "what is our purpose"? "What are we really doing?" "What should we be doing?" "What's stopping us from getting on with the work that we know really matters?"

In their groundbreaking studies of Canadian competitiveness, *Canada at the Crossroads*, and its successor, *Canadian Competitiveness: Nine Years after the Crossroads*, Roger Martin and Michael Porter argued that Canada needed to embrace "relentless innovation" and "bold strategy" if the country was to succeed in the modern economy[x]. In business, government, the arts, and other aspects of civil society – in Canada and elsewhere, we need to resist the temptation to "play it safe" and do what others do. From time-to-time, being a fast follower can work, but in general we need to foster an organizational, if not societal culture in which risk taking is good, in which new ideas are celebrated, in which undiscovered voices are heard. Where, after all, will bold innovation come from? Anybody can have 1 good idea, but how do you create the conditions in which good ideas – and the translation of those ideas into tangible products and services – are a self-reinforcing virtuous circle? Put another way, what is your competitive advantage, and what are you doing, today, to ensure it's sustainable? And how do we couple what I will call the sustainability agenda with the economic and innovation agenda? Sustainability, after all, isn't just about reducing pollution or building stronger social connections; it's about the scientific research that drives the creation of new companies and new economic opportunities. It's about the way we design and build communities to maximize livability for local residents, and become a magnet for visitors. For too long we have treated these objectives and aspirations as disparate ideas. They're not; they are part of an integrated whole.

Transparency in business is a trend that has been gathering steam in the wake of the Wall Street scandals of 2002, but its roots extend further back. Kevin Kelly has long talked about the "new economy" being built on chips and trust - the engines of economic growth may be changing, but you still need the trust of your community to survive, much less prosper. Interbrand, a leading international brand consultancy, has extended the argument and pointed out that by 2010 intangibles could account for 45% of a company's market capitalization[xi]. This raises exciting and challenging possibilities for business. How are you going to create value in a world where physical assets don't count as much as they used to, where intangibles are gold, and where trust (or lack thereof) can overturn strategic positions very quickly?

Finally, and perhaps most importantly, we need to accelerate the transition in business from a purely shareholder value model to what Ed Freeman and others call "stakeholder value" or "stakeholder capitalism". This is about creating value for all stakeholders, not simply those who invested in the company. This requires that we redefine how we think about and measure success. It also requires that we understand the importance of trust and transparency in business.

Unless we all learn to reflect more; define a clear and compelling sense of purpose; take more risks; operate more transparently; and emphasize value beyond the shareholder there's probably room for improvement in our lives and the lives of the companies we serve. The collection that follows explores this proposition in more detail.

Notes to Introduction

[i] The term "sustainable" was first used by the Germans in the 18th century to describe a long-term perspective in forestry. In its more recent connotation, sustainable (and its close cousins, sustainability and sustainable development) has been defined more broadly. For example, the Canadian International Development Agency (CIDA) has argued that "...in addition to education, health, employment and environment, sustainable development is also about respect and equity, justice and democracy, fair access to resources and having a voice in shaping your own future (*Globe and Mail*, May 27, 2003).

[ii] As the economic recession deepens in the early months of 2009 the fragility of the boom is being cast into sharp relief – some fossil fuel energy companies have disappeared, layoffs have been announced, and investment in the heavy oil deposits of northern Alberta (the so-called "oil sands") will likely be reduced by 50% in 2009.

[iii] Schindler, the Killam Memorial Professor of Ecology at the University of Alberta, believes that decreases in the quality and quantity of Canada's freshwater supply might be the largest crisis facing the country in the 21st century.

[iv] In a recent blog, Kunstler underscored the urgency of our plight. "We have to get off of petro-agriculture and grow our own food locally, at a smaller scale, with more people working on it and fewer machines. This is an enormous project, which implies change in everything from property allocation to farming methods to new social relations. But if we don't focus on it right away, a lot of Americans will end up starving, and rather soon.

[v] There are signs that human society might yet shift to a relationship with the Earth that is more sustainable. In their book, *Natural Capitalism*, Paul Hawken, Amory Lovins and Hunter Lovins celebrated the many rapidly emerging principles, codes and other frameworks that collectively hold the promise of whole-system thinking (and whole system change), and a consensus from the breadth of society rather than its ruling structures. My earlier book, *Uncommon Cents: Thoreau and the Nature of Business*, discusses many of these examples – hopeful signs of a course change, especially on the part of business.

[vi] Of particular interest for the practitioner or student is the effort to create what Michael Porter and Jay Barney (and others) have elegantly described as "sustained competitive advantage" (SCA). A firm achieves SCA when it is implementing a value creating strategy that is not being simultaneously implemented by a competitor and when this competing firm is unable to duplicate the benefits of the strategy.

[vii] The MEA website is an excellent (and sobering) source of information on the state of natural capital on the planet – www.millenniumassessment.org.

[viii] North America's Big 3 automakers come readily to mind here; what if they hadn't resisted radical green innovation? What if they had engaged their employees – both those still working and those who had retired – in strategic conversations about a new kind of labor arrangement? It is easy to armchair quarterback this particular industry from the vantage point of 2009, and I don't want to push things too far, but it seems clear to me that a greater degree of reflection would have generated a different and better outcome for the companies and their stakeholders.

[ix] See Charles Handy, "What's a Business For?" in the *Harvard Business Review*, December 2002, pp. 49-55.

[x] In the November 10, 2008 edition of BusinessWeek, Porter applied the same logic in a masterful essay, "Why America Needs an Economic Strategy". He says the "stark truth is that the U.S. has no long-term economic strategy—no coherent set of policies to ensure competitiveness over the long haul. Strategy embodies clear priorities, based on understanding the strengths we need to preserve and the weaknesses that threaten our prosperity the most. Strategy addresses what to do, but also what not to do. In dealing with a crisis, experience teaches us that steps to address the immediate problem must support a long-term strategy. Yet it is far from clear that we are taking the steps most important to America's long-term economic prosperity".

[xi] In addition, the Rotman School of Management at the University of Toronto estimates that 40% to 60% pf a firm's total brand value is now based on envirohmental and social performance.

Origins

The major problems of the world are the result of the difference between the way nature works and the way men think.

—Gregory Bateson

With time comes perspective. And with perspective comes an appreciation for the memories that sustain us. My family lived in the country when I was a child, near the banks of the Oyster River on Vancouver Island, and my father would take me to the river's edge to fish, to watch, to listen. "Much that is important in life can only be learned here", he said. Wild roses grew alongside the river and these were especially important to him. They were confirmation that he was in the right place. He had moved to the country to raise a family and create a new life away from the city. He wanted his wife and children to experience nature and hopefully, come to appreciate it as he did. He wanted, as Thoreau would have it, "to live deliberately, to front only the essential facts of life". I remember those now distant afternoons by the river. I remember the heat of the sand, the smell of the water and wild roses. I can feel the water bending around my legs, and I can see him, for all time, smiling in the moment. We would sit there among the roses and read, pausing to listen to the river. In time, my love of words and books would grow to rival his own and we would spend long hours talking about the books we were reading, or wanted to read. The Ruba'iyat of Omar Khayyam was one of his favorites:

If the heart could grasp the meaning of life,
In death it would know the mystery of God;

Today when you are in possession of yourself, you know nothing.
Tomorrow when you leave yourself behind, what will you know?
Neither you nor I know the mysteries of eternity,
Neither you nor I read this enigma;
You and I only talk this side of the veil;
When the veil falls, neither you nor I will be here.
The cycle which includes our coming and going
Has no discernible beginning nor end;
Nobody has got this matter straight –
Where we come from and where we go to.

Every summer we camped in the headwaters of the river. Today when I recall those trips, when I share the memories with friends, they marvel that we could camp for two weeks and never see another person. And I am reminded again of how precious those memories are to me. In A River Runs Through It, Norman MacLean talks of the Montana hillsides and riverbanks of his youth being a world with the dew still on it. To appreciate what he means, you must soak your feet and legs in grass laden with early morning dew and watch the mist rise from a river. You must splash the water from that river onto your face and revel in the sensation of the river in your body and on your skin. It is a world that never sleeps, and if you are lucky, as I was, you can live in it.

Thirty-two years after I first tasted the river my father loved, I stood on its banks with my mother and brother and scattered his ashes. In that moment when his physical self was returned to the river, my life dissolved to our shared experiences and the memories that have informed the person I am, and might yet become: discovering what we now call the hydro riparian ecosystem by exploring the riverbank, especially at twilight; finding dry firewood under a stump in the middle of a downpour; improvising a rain poncho from a plastic tablecloth; learning to cast a dry fly; and the telling of stories around the campfire. I gave back his physical self that day; his spiritual, transcendent self will be with me always. He died knowing that he had lived, knowing that he had learned from nature what it had to teach…

Reflection and Renewal on the Road to Valhalla[1]

Northrop Frye, Canada's (and arguably the world's) seminal literary critic and theorist, once observed that early settlers feared the Canadian environment and this fear spurred domination and exploitation. Margaret Atwood, the celebrated Canadian novelist, poet, essayist and critic, has also examined the "malevolent north" in Canadian literature[i] and how it has shaped our attitudes toward our land and culture. I thought of all this earlier this summer as Canadians (how many, I wonder?) celebrated Environment Week.

It is now more than 30 years since British Columbia MP Tom Goode introduced a Private Members Bill in the Canadian House of Commons inaugurating Environment Week. Why do we still need a weeklong event to remind us to think about the environmental consequences of our lifestyle? Is there a large constituency that still views the environment with fear and suspicion, as something to be dominated? Fear and suspicion are probably not the right sentiment. Neglect and lack of awareness seem closer to the mark. And because of this lack of awareness we need Environment Week more than ever, albeit with a renewed focus.

On May 27, 2003 the results of a national nature audit by the World Wildlife Fund (WWF) indicated that Canada's natural resources and wild ecosystems are under intense pressure from human settlements and a concerted effort is needed to prevent further erosion of our natural capital. I use the word capital in this context deliberately – our capacity as individuals, firms and a society to create social and economic wealth, or well being, to create quality of life, is inextricably

[1] This piece was first written and posted online (www.abbottstrategies.com) in June of 2003. It has been revised for this publication. Further, the use of "Valhalla" in the title is deliberate; in Norse mythology, this was the grand hall in which the souls of heros slain in battle were received by Odin. Human society is waging a battle of its own – quite different in some respects from the battle waged by Norse warriors, but similar in others. If we make the right choices, the right sacrifices, our souls may find lasting peace in our own "Valhalla".

linked to the natural world. Moreover, nature provides essential life-support services for which there is no human-made substitute. The regulation of the composition of the atmosphere or the cycling of nutrients comes readily to mind. Viewed in this light, the WWF findings are disturbing. And WWF isn't alone. A study released in 2002 by the Eco-Research Chair of Environmental Law and Policy at the University of Victoria placed Canada 28th out of 29 OECD countries in environmental performance[ii]. The Millennium Ecosystem Assessment has since updated the state of natural capital within the OECD and extended the assessment to the planet as a whole. The results are not encouraging[iii]:

> Human activities are depleting Earth's natural capital and putting such strain on the environment that the ability of the planet's ecosystem to sustain future generations can no longer be taken for granted.

The Montreal-based writer, Taras Grescoe recently used the world's oceans as a lens through which to graphically chronicle the steady, and not so steady, decline of the natural world[iv]:

> It is a multigenerational, continent-spanning tale with a narrative arc as relentless as anything written by Hardy or Zola, one that documents the decline of the oceans from a recent past of prelapsarian plenty to a near future of unimaginable barrenness.
>
> The storyline of this saga is simple, the facts stark. The action starts on the North Atlantic 200 years ago, when pre-industrial fishing communities relying on wooden-hulled vessels and sail power exploited, but did not seriously deplete, the oceans as a source of food. The change comes in increments, with the adoption of bottom-trawlers, well boats and steam engines. Even as the first populations of flatfish are being fished to extinction, and the fishermen of Whitby and Grimsby are forced north to Iceland, Victorian hubris and hyperbole hold that human efforts can never seriously affect

> the world's "cod mountains" and endlessly self-renewing salmon rivers.
>
> The industrial techniques pioneered on the North Sea are exported to the Grand Banks, the North Pacific and Asia. Stern trawlers the size of destroyers, purse-seiners that can encircle a dozen nuclear submarines, sonar, spotter planes, GPS, and DuPont's nylon monofilament netting become the norm. Equipped with the latest technology, the fishing fleets of the world become armadas facing enemies with brains the size of chickpeas.
>
> By the turn of the millennium, 90 per cent of the world's predator fish – tuna, sharks, swordfish – have been removed from the ocean; leading marine ecologists to project that, because of pollution, climate change and overfishing, all the world's major fisheries will collapse within the next 50 years. The saga ends where it began, in North Atlantic fishing towns, where the locals are reduced to catching slime eels and tourists in search of the quaint get served farmed-in-China tilapia at local seafood shacks.

It should hardly come as a surprise, then, that the American painter, Alexis Rockman, has attracted much attention for his outsize works depicting a post-apocalyptic yet all too foreseeable future[v]. In *Manifest Destiny*, his 8-by-24 foot oil painting of the Brooklyn Bridge several centuries from now, a rising tropical sea submerges the ruined bridge abutments. And in *Bathos*, he portrays Wall Street as an underwater "urban reef" after a rise in sea levels[vi]. Lest the reader think Rockman's work is little more than artistic flights of fancy, Eugene Linden reminds us in *The Future in Plain Sight* that:

> Around the world, an estimated three hundred million people are directly at risk from a one-meter rise in the oceans. Should the world see more frequent and intense storms in the coming years, hundreds of millions more stand to suffer, since thirty of the world's fifty largest cities lie near coasts.

And the Indian scientist and economist, Rajendra Pachauri, who accepted the Nobel Peace Prize on behalf of the Intergovernmental Panel of Climate Change in 2007, said that "if there's no action before 2012, that's too late. What we do in the next two to three years will determine our future. This is the defining moment".

As individuals, firms and a society we need to ask some searching questions about why our ecosystems are still in retreat, why lifestyle choices continue to run against the environment. Early in 2003, in what can now be seen as a bell weather sign that it's truly not easy being green, The Globe and Mail reported that the 3 cars Environmental Defense Canada rated the "greenest" were among the poorest-selling. Why is that? Have we failed to get the price signals right? Maybe, but I suspect there are other, more complex forces at play. Despite much rhetoric (and to be fair, some genuinely well-intentioned policy), we have not made the connections between environmental quality and social or economic wellbeing meaningful to a sufficiently large number of Canadians. We have also, as Ronald Wright reminds us, not learned from history:

> Like Gauguin, we often prefer to think of the deep past as innocent and unspoiled, a time of ease and simple plenty before a fall from paradise. The words "Eden" and "Paradise" feature prominently in the titles of popular books on anthropology and history. For some, Eden was the pre-agricultural world, the age of hunting and gathering; for others, it was the pre-Columbian world, the Americas before the white man; and for many, it was the pre-industrial world, the long stillness before the machine. Certainly there have been good and bad times to be alive. But the truth is that human beings drove themselves out of Eden, and they have done it again and again by fouling their own nests.

Wright deftly points out that before the time of Christ, the poet, Ovid observed:

> Long ago…
> No one tore the ground with ploughshares

or parcelled out the land
or swept the sea with dipping oars –
the shore was the world's end.
Clever human nature, victim of your inventions,
disastrously creative,
why cordon cities with towered walls?
Why arm for war?

It is to this task – learning from history and making the connections between human survival and environmental integrity more obvious to significantly more people – that Environment Week and events like it across Canada should now turn. How can we catalyze genuine discourse, and with it, genuine progress? How can we couple progress, if not transformation, in our approach to environmental and social concerns with an innovative scientific and economic agenda?

And it's not just in Canada that we need to question the sincerity of our commitment to the little (and not so little) changes that are the cornerstone of a sustainable society. In the June 15, 2003 edition of the *New York Times Magazine*, Elinor Burkett pointed out that Cape Wind Associates' proposal to build America's first offshore wind farm, something that is old hat in Europe, was being vigorously opposed by the good people of Nantucket Sound. Despite the fact that the wind farm would provide Cape Cod residents with up to 75% of their electricity, these erstwhile Greens have put aside their environmental sensitivities and are demanding that their homes be exempt from such a project[vii]. Plus ca change...

Wendell Berry has said that if we were sincerely looking for "success" as a society, we would turn to the communities of which we are a part – humanity, water, earth, air, plants and animals. Put another way, we would forsake our individual lives of affluence and remember that what really matters are the choices we make everyday to help ourselves and each other. And therein lays the crux of the sustainability challenge – how do we deliver the utility people want in a way that respects the hopes and aspirations of others? How do we make the connections between our daily lives and the natural world, which should be obvious, more immediate and immediately important, to more people? How do we live with a lighter footprint, but larger hearts? I don't pretend to have all the answers yet, but I am consumed by these questions.

Ecological Integrity and the Green Business Hypothesis: A Tiger by the Tale[2]

Concern for the environment is not new. In a North American, if not global context the organizational and ideological roots of environmentalism can be traced to the progressive conservation movement of the late 19th century that emerged in response to the perceived exploitation of natural resources[viii]. The result of this initial environmental concern on the North American continent was a series of conferences and conventions that are notable for at least two reasons. First, they provided a forum to discuss natural resource use policy, including policy alternatives to the prevailing doctrine of usefulness[ix]. Second, they raised many of the same issues that resource and environmental managers continue to debate today. The North American Conservation Conference in 1909, for example, resulted in a Declaration of Principles that called for "legislation to preserve and protect wildlife, to prevent soil erosion and water pollution, and generally to manage renewable resources in such a way as to ensure their continued productivity in the future".

The energy and enthusiasm of these early policy discussions abated with the onset of World War I, but they left a legacy of ideas, organizations and government agencies. Notable examples in the US are the Sierra Club, the National Audubon Society, the National Park Service, and the Forest Service. The next substantive wave of environmental concern emerged in the 1960s, propelled in part by the *Resources for Tomorrow Conference* (1961), the disclosures of Rachel Carson's masterwork, *Silent Spring* (1962), and the efforts of the Sierra Club to call attention to threats to natural beauty. This period marked an ideological shift toward conservation and environmental management. The birth of the modern environmental movement is typically

---

2 I was first exposed to some of the ideas in this paper while a graduate student at the University of Toronto's Institute for Environmental Studies in the 1980s. I have subsequently developed them into the piece included here. Dr. Robert France has been helpful in refining my thinking about option strategies for ecological protection.

marked by the Earth Day celebrations of April 22, 1970. Two years later, the United Nations Conference on the Human Environment and The Club of Rome's controversial book, *The Limits to Growth*, consolidated human concern about the deterioration of the environment and unconstrained resource consumption .

In the years since these watershed events, perceptions and attitudes toward the environment have continued to evolve. As Frances Cairncross ably pointed out in *Costing the Earth*, the 1970s and 1980s were periods of extensive regulation, directed primarily at domestic issues such as water quality and hazardous waste. The introduction of these regulations, often with little explicit acknowledgement or understanding of the cost of implementing them, was supported by a succession of high profile environmental incidents in the mid-to-late-1980s that galvanized societal concern about the presence and effectiveness of environmental management programs in industry. These included:

- The escape of toxic gas from a Union Carbide pesticide plant in Bhopal, India (1985) that killed over 3,000 people
- The identification of a hole in the ozone layer above Antarctica (1985),
- A reactor accident at the Chernobyl nuclear station that released 7 tons of radioactive material (1986)
- A chemical spill from a Sandoz plant in Switzerland that severely damaged the Rhine River (1986)
- The murder of rainforest activist Chico Mendes by Brazilian ranchers (1988)
- The Exxon Valdez oil spill in Prince William Sound, Alaska (1989)

The 1990s saw a third ideological shift. Recognition of the global nature of environmental problems and an increased acceptance of ecological interdependence introduced new language to the environmental debate, notably the concept of sustainability. And so it is that planning and decision-making frameworks to foster sustainability have been undertaken in many countries. Early examples included Holland's National Environmental Policy Plan, *To Choose or to Lose*, the UK's

White Paper, *This Common Inheritance*, and *Sustainable Development: The UK Strategy*, Japan's *New Earth 21*, and the European Commission's Fifth Environmental Action Program, *Toward Sustainability*. The 2050 Project, a collaborative venture involving the World Resources Institute, the Brookings Institution, and the Sante Fe Institute, is an attempt to define the conditions under which global society could be sustainable in 2050 and is reflective of the change in environmental thinking and planning. So too, is the 2030 Project, an effort undertaken by the Sustainable Development Research Institute at the University of British Columbia that attempted to model environmental change in the Lower Mainland region of British Columbia over four decades and facilitate improved environmental decision making[xi]. The underlying theme that links these activities, apart from a focus on global issues and ecological interdependence, is an increased willingness on the part of government, industry, and other stakeholders to examine the role that environmental management can play in business and strategic planning. The environment is no longer seen solely as a scientific, technical or engineering issue; it is also seen as a strategic issue that can potentially shape broad government and corporate policy, and separate winners from losers in business. It is an exciting time, but the sustainability era is still in its early stages and the way ahead is not clear. How can business and industry institutionalize sustainability? What is the most efficient and effective route to sustainability? Like the explorers of old, society is moving into unmapped territory – the terra incognita of human knowledge.

Against this backdrop, table 1 summarizes a combined option-strategy protocol that may serve as a compass to assist business in becoming sustainable. It reflects earlier work by Robert France and illustrates how ideas and approaches in one field may inform the development of solutions in another. For too long we have been mired in work that is typical of "slowing the rate of retreat", "holding the line", or at best, "incremental advances". For too long we have lived under the intellectual yoke that says environmental performance improvement is a drag on business efficiency and competitiveness. For too long we have ignored the essential fact of our existence – that we are part of nature. The time has truly come for us to realize that we need to engage in what is described in table 1 as partial and deep reform. We need to create new rules for business and society and begin creating a future that is sustainable.

Table 1: Combined Option-Strategy Protocol for Business Sustainability

Integrity Level	Extent of Reform	Escaped Tiger Level	Management Action for Business Sustainability
1.	Deep Reform	Prevent energy marshalling (1)	Business transformation: - Radical resource productivity - Closed loop production - Solutions-based business - Protection of natural capital
		Reduce energy marshalling (2)	Programs to systematically reduce negative environmental and social impacts - social audits as well as environmental - overall resource efficiency improved - economic measures broaden
		Prevent energy release (3)	Thinking about environmental management broadens to embrace sustainability: - improve resource productivity - protect natural capital - invest in social capital
2.	Partial Reform	Modify rate or spatial scale of energy release (4)	Programs to reduce environmental footprint of business. Some thinking about social capital
		Time/space separation of energy release (5)	Pollution prevention programs. Closed loop production as evolution of EMS
3.	Incremental Advances	Separation by barrier interposition (6)	Develop EMS to international standard (ISO 14001). Begin to question where and how environmental activity can support business objectives
		Modify contact surface (7)	Develop environmental management system (EMS). Awareness of business "footprint"
		Return to pre-event and stabilization of altered state (10)	Comply with law (or try to)
4.	Holding the Line	Strengthen structure (8)	Develop audit programs. Beginning of systems thinking
5.	Slowing the Rate of Retreat	Generation of signal in response to damage (9)	Ad hoc programs for "key" environmental risks (those that are visible or regulated). Monitoring and measuring, but not linked to business planning
		Return to pre-event and stabilization of altered state (10)	Comply with law (or try to)

In his celebrated paper from 1990, *Environmental Management in Development: The Evolution of Paradigms*, Michael Colby observed that behavioral and cultural factors retard change, despite economic imperatives:

> It is possible that by restructuring along the lines of eco-development, companies and economies might develop new comparative advantages that will help to make those that are quickest to adjust more competitive and prosperous in the long run, rather than less so, as is frequently heard today. Some developing countries might even be able to "leapfrog" over the "environmental protection" phase to a much more sustainable as well as self-defined state of development.

Many environmental activities and events have taken place since Coby's paper, events that have done much to overcome behavioral and cultural barriers to environmental improvement. An equal measure of diligence for the foreseeable future on practical tools that improve environmental planning and decision making will help society collectively achieve the sustainable future that Colby envisioned. This combined option-strategy protocol for business sustainability is a modest contribution in this regard.

Sustainability and the Search for an Epistemological Sword[3]

Setting the Stage

Can it really be nearly three decades since the inaugural Earth Day? As one who grew up in the modern environmental movement, I still hear echoes of Aldo Leopold and Rachel Carson directing us to protect the world around us, to move society onto a different road, a different trajectory. But these echoes are of a time that is a distant memory, part of our history. The intervening years have seen much to celebrate, but perhaps even more to fear. The Union of Concerned Scientists, a group of 1,600 that includes 100 Nobel Laureates, sounded a stern warning in 1992 that society has was trending toward global ecological and social collapse:

Human beings and the natural world are on a collision course. Human activities inflict harsh and often irreversible damage on the environment and on critical resources. If not checked, many of our current practices put at serious risk the future that we wish for human society and the plant and animal kingdoms, and may so alter the living world that it will be unable to sustain life in the manner that we know. Fundamental changes are urgent if we are to avoid the collision our present course will bring about.

The Royal Society (UK), the National Academy of Scientists (US), and many others have voiced similar warnings. Against this grim backdrop it seems timely to comment on the arguments put forth by advocates who suggest that sustainability is the "road less traveled by". While these advocates are, for the moment at least, united by their belief in sustainability, the emphasis in their arguments is strikingly different. Economists argue that an enlightened sense of price, of the value of the ecological world, is all that is needed to reverse the trend

[3] This piece was first written in 1998 while undertaking Doctoral studies at Simon Fraser's University's School of Resource of Environmental Management. It has been revised and expanded for this collection.

of ecological degradation. Technocrats are not impressed and believe that human ingenuity is the answer. Still others, spiritual descendents of Thoreau perhaps, believe that a fundamental shift in society's ethics will do more for sustainability than anything else. Let us consider each of these perspectives in turn.

Wait a Minute, Technology Can Fix That!

To suggest that technology can lead society onto a sustainable path is to invite scorn. After all, hasn't the industrial economy, and the technology that drives it, caused so much of the environmental degradation and social dislocation around us? Paul Gray, the former president of the Massachusetts Institute of Technology, calls this the paradox of technological development; technology causes environmental damage, but it can also repair that damage. The reparation includes the creation of substitutes for scarce natural resources, the development of more efficient products that allow existing resources to be stretched further, and perhaps most important, the institution of new ways of thinking about the world. C.S. (Buzz) Holling, cites the reconstruction of the composition of the Earth's atmosphere using bubbles trapped in the Vostok ice core from Antarctica and its correlation with climate using proxy biological and chemical signals as a particularly exciting contribution to the sustainability debate[xii]. As he puts it:

> It is also useful for politicians. It tells them that the present concentration of carbon dioxide in our atmosphere is higher than it has been for the last 160,000 years.

Satellite imagery, remote sensing, and geographic information systems are additional forms of technology that have made significant recent contributions to human understanding of planetary functions, notably biophysical processes that operate over an enormous scale. Moreover, rapid advances in artificial intelligence allow different types of knowledge to be logically considered in the search for better, more sustainable decisions about resource use and environmental protection. Moving from understanding to application, heat pumps, space-conditioning control systems, high efficiency lighting, and advanced recycling technologies are already helping to steer society toward sustainability.

A familiar example underscores the merits of the technological path to sustainability. Fax machines transmit documents electronically using one-half to one-seventh of the primary energy needed to send a letter by postal or courier service. More pointedly, the energy from a barrel of oil can send roughly 25,000 pages by courier, but if converted to electricity to run a fax machine, can send 175,000 pages. The emergence of e-mail is arguably even more sustainable than fax technology as it reduces paper consumption – if the e-mails are not printed.

Many of the technological innovations that facilitate sustainability are already here, what is needed is the will to use them more creatively. For example, low temperature superconductors and microprocessors are increasing the efficiency with which electricity is transmitted, stored and used commercially; the same technology could help to optimize residential electrical use by integrating appliances and exploiting off-peak power.

Quite apart from levering existing technology to other quarters, there is an opportunity to develop and commercialize new technologies, what John Elkington calls "super innovations" which re-shape social possibilities. Two examples are the electric car and the hypercar. The Sacramento Municipal Utility District (SMUD), as part of an integrated sustainable energy strategy, operates a fleet of over 100 electric vehicles[xiii]- recharged by solar energy, and Amory Lovins of the Rocky Mountain Institute has demonstrated the feasibility of hypercars. The latter are fully recyclable, twenty times more energy efficient, and one hundred times cleaner than existing cars. They retain the safety and performance of conventional cars but achieve radical simplification through the use of lightweight, composite materials, fewer parts, virtual prototyping, regenerative braking, and small, hybrid engines. The Department of Energy (US) is sufficiently committed to electric vehicles as a sustainability option that it has established a hybrid electric vehicle propulsion program, and has subcontracts with General Motors, Ford and Chrysler to produce production feasible electric vehicles.

There is a tendency to fear technology, to run from what Edward Tenner calls technology's "revenge effect". This fear, which is very real, is a good thing. It is a check on unrestrained technology, but it should not be used as justification to straightjacket technology and rely on an economic system that has treated the environment with malignant neglect, or societal ethics that change, if at all, very slowly. Life cycle assessment and product stewardship are increasingly being used to screen prospective technologies and identify those that are sustainable.

The Price is Right: Economics to the Rescue

Economists smile in the face of the technological argument because the best way of applying technology to the resolution of environmental problems is to "get the price signals right". If prices do not reflect the true cost of using environmental resources, companies and households will not value the environment as they value labor and capital and they will not be interested in increasing their productivity in the use of the environment, through technology or any other means. For the economist, the issue is not to rely on technology, or ethics for that matter, but to acknowledge, as Barry Field and Nancy Olewiler point out in their fine introductory text, *Environmental Economics*, that "people pollute because it's the cheapest way they have of solving a certain very practical problem...the disposal of the waste products remaining after consumers have finished using something, or after businesses have finished producing something." Technology and ethics are details; important details to be sure, but not the crux of the sustainability debate.

The economists' argument, at least in part, says that society makes decisions with respect to production, consumption, and disposal within socially prescribed institutions - markets, corporations, commercial law, public agencies - that provide incentives for behavior. To move toward sustainability, you don't need technology or ethics, you need to change the institutions and incentives. And so it is that taxes, subsidies, and tradable emission permits are receiving increasing play as economic levers for sustainability. As Tom Tietenberg put it:

> "Instead of mandating prescribed actions, such as requiring the installation of a particular piece of control equipment, this

> approach achieves environmental objectives by changing the economic incentives of the agents. By changing the incentives an individual agent faces, that agent can use his typically superior information to select the best means of meeting his assigned responsibility. Among other virtues, approaches relying on economic incentives can reduce the conflict between environmental protection and economic development, can ease the transition to a sustainable (rather than exploitative) relationship between the economy and the environment, and can encourage the development of new, more environmentally benign production processes."

In addition to the deployment of economic incentives, there is another part of the economic argument that is particularly interesting. Here, proponents such as Herman Daly, John Cobb Jr., and Robert Costanza stake out new ground by arguing that growth and development should not be confused, as so many sustainability pundits have done. "When something grows it gets bigger, when something develops it gets different". The economy must eventually stop growing, but it can, and should, continue to develop by shifting to conceptions of wealth that are defined not by conventional metrics but by a throughput of matter-energy that is within the regenerative and assimilative capacities of the ecosystem. This line of thinking springs from a belief that economic indicators such as gross domestic product do not accurately reflect social welfare. Frances Cairncross underlined this point in Costing the Earth:

> When a forest is cut down and sold, the country appears to grow richer - even though the trees may not be replaced, and their removal may result in soil erosion, flooding and the loss of food and fuel gathered by local people.

Daly and others are leading economics into a new and exciting future that includes more than incentives to internalize environmental and social costs. They are forging a dialogue around new measures of wealth and prosperity, and in doing so are positioning economics as a compass to guide society onto a sustainable path[xiv]. Steve Lerner, in

Eco-Pioneers, his wide-ranging examination of sustainability in the United States, summarized the challenge and opportunity of economics in this context:

> Looking ahead it appears as if two significant changes must take place if we are to establish a more sustainable culture in the United States. First, we must shift the way we price goods and services to reflect more accurately their environmental costs. And second, we must develop a context within which commerce can take place within the limits of nature. Changing our laws, taxes, regulations, subsidies and economic indicators so that they promote sustainable activities now looms as the great task of the environmental movement.

It's an Ethical Question: Who Should Speak for the Earth?

If economists smile at the technologists, those who believe that ethics lie at the core of sustainability shake their collective head at any alternative proposition - much in the manner of a patient grandparent watching children in a playground. They view technology and economics as tools perhaps, but the blueprint is societal ethics. To achieve sustainability, the argument goes, you must foster an ethical awakening. For example, rising "consumer confidence" is routinely used as a surrogate for a prosperous economy even though the associated spending may have depleted natural resources and increased waste – and household debt[xv]. It is therefore necessary to re-educate society with respect to prosperity. Of particular importance is the need to change what can only charitably be called the consumption "ethic". The scientist, philosopher and scholar, Nicholas Georgescu-Roegen highlighted the dangers thusly:

> Once man expanded his biological powers by means of industrial artifacts, he became ipso facto not only dependent on a very scarce source of life support but also addicted to industrial luxuries. It is as if the human species were determined to have a short but exciting life.

Ethics that support consumerism and continued economic growth are a formidable adversary to proponents of sustainability. In a powerful article published in the September 23rd 1998 edition of *The Globe and Mail*, Nobel Laureate, Nadine Gordimer reported that global advertising spending exceeded $435 billion (US) - more than five times the total annual income of all people in the poorest countries of the world[xvi]. In the face of such an advertising blitz, you cannot rely on economic instruments or technology to chart a sustainable course, you need to change the way people think and the way they respond to such advertising. This will require changes to the education system that foster new generations of environmentally literate people. These educational efforts should point out that society is losing its endowment of natural resources and that societal change is necessary to arrest these losses. A new ethic that emphasizes non-material rather than material satisfaction, cooperation, and the recognition that society must live within its financial and ecological limits to protect a finite world are needed. This is also, by the way, what James Kunstler means when he talks about the need to be citizens rather than consumers. Citizens have rights, but they also have responsibilities to the commons. Failure to remember that, and practice that responsibility, imperils us all.

One of the interesting, and encouraging, features of the ethical argument is that it is not being driven exclusively by government, non-governmental organizations, or even concerned citizens. The business community, long the shadowy nemesis of the environmental movement, is playing an active role in the cultivation of a new competitive ethos. The International Chamber of Commerce (www.iccwbo.org), the World Business Council for Sustainable Development (www.wbcsd.org), and the Global Environmental Management Initiative (www.gemi.org) are all high-profile examples of business organizations that are shifting the ethics, the values, and the beliefs of their members. The most striking example, however, comes from the World Business Academy (www.worldbusiness.org). The WBA is an international body of business leaders whose purpose is to forge an international dialogue about how businesses, as socially prescribed institutions, can foster a "sane, humane and ecologically sound global future". The ideas espoused by the WBA, and the notion that business might be part of the sustainability solution is new and refreshing. The old societal model is imperfect and no amount of technology or economics is going to correct it. A new ethical perspective is the prism needed to see the world in a new, sustainable, light.

So Who's Right?

To ask the question is, in some respects, to miss the point. Each of the perspectives is tempting, and therein lies the fundamental challenge for society. To choose one over the others is to foreclose important opportunity. The trick, or art, is to use all three of these perspectives in new and creative ways. Technology has some undeniable merit, but we must be wary of unintended side effects and the potential for efficiency gains to be offset by increased consumption. Economics has exciting potential, but is still bedeviled by the difficulty of identifying environmental and social costs (and benefits). Finally, few would argue with the desirability of moving society onto a "better" ethical plane, but even if agreement could be reached on what is "better", such changes will not be reached quickly. The way ahead should therefore be based on an integrated approach in which society searches for opportunities where technology is particularly well suited - the understanding of planetary functions, for example - coupled to selected economic solutions that encourage technology investment and supported by efforts directed at ethical awakening. Such a pluralistic approach acknowledges that the world around us is the most complex of systems and cannot be understood, must less managed, using one tool, technique or perspective.

In the ancient world, Alexander the Great was confronted with a seemingly intractable problem, the Gordian knot. Unlike so many before him who had failed by using conventional logic and tools, he looked at the problem from a different perspective, resolved it quickly, and secured his future. As we contemplate the prospect of shifting society onto a more sustainable plane, we would do well to forge our own epistemological sword through an appreciation of the interplay of technology, economics and ethics and learn where and how to use such an instrument. This is also what Al Gore means when he talks of the rare opportunity our global plight affords us:

> The climate crisis also offers us the chance to experience what very few generations in history have had the privilege of knowing: a generational mission; the exhilaration of a compelling moral purpose; a shared and unifying cause; the thrill of being forced by circumstances to put aside the pettiness and conflict that so often stifle the restless human need for transcendence; the opportunity to rise.

The opportunity to rise, to transcend. Seems like a reasonable toll to travel on the road less traveled by, no?

Notes to Section 1

[i] See, for example, Northrop Frye's essay collection, *The Bush Garden* (House of Anansi Press, 1995), which describes the "looming wilderness of the north" and observes, "The Wordsworth who saw nature as exquisitely fitted to the human mind would be lost in Canada." Margaret Atwood's essay collection, *Strange Things: The Malevolent North in Canadian Literature* (Oxford University Press, 1996), continues her exploration of this topic, begun with her superb and influential 1972 book, *Survival: A Thematic Guide to Canadian Literature*. In *Strange Things*, Atwood focuses on three themes: (1) the "devouring implacable, direly feminine North" as expressed in literary treatments of John Franklin's 1840s attempt to navigate the Northwest Passage; (2) the impulse to "go native", perhaps best exemplified by the story of Grey Owl, an English expatriate who assumed the identity of a Canadian Indian; and (3) the ice-hearted, human flesh-eating monster, the Wendigo. American readers will be interested in Roderick Nash's hugely influential book from 1967, *Wilderness and the American Mind*, in which he documents a cultural evolution with respect to wilderness. The early settlers, charged with the Judeo-Christian belief system, sought to subdue wilderness or "the frontier". With time, this feeling changed to one of appreciation for wilderness. More recent examinations of the topic in the US context include *The Great New Wilderness Debate* (1998, University of Georgia Press), and *American Wilderness: A New History* (2007, Oxford University Press).

[ii] See David Boyd's 2001 report, Canada vs. the OECD: An Environmental Comparison, published by the University of Victoria Eco-Chair of Environmental Law and Policy.

[iii] Seven specific findings are worthy of mention here: (1) Over the past 50 years, humans have changed ecosystems more rapidly and extensively than in any comprable period of time in human history; (2) the changes that have been made to ecosystems have contributed to net gains in human well being and economic development, but these gains have come at the cost of ecosystem degradation; (3) approximately 60 per cent of the ecosystem services examined are being degraded or used unsustainably; (4) the full costs of the loss and degradation of ecosystem services are difficult

to measure, but the available evidence suggests that they are substantial and growing; (5) the harmful effects of this degradation are being borne disproportionately by the poor; (6) the degradation of ecosystem services is already a significant barrier to achieving the Millennium Development Goals; and (7) there is established but incomplete evidence that changes being made in ecosystems are increasing the likelihood of non-linear changes (accelerating, abrupt and potentially irreversible changes) that have important consequences for human well being.

[iv] Charles Clover painted a similarly grim picture in his excellent 2004 book, *The End of Line*: "Fish were once seen as renewable resources, creatures that would replenish their stocks forever for our benefit. But around the world there is evidence that numerous types of fish are not recovering. Reassurances from official sources on both sides of the Atlantic that the seas are being 'managed' scientifically is increasingly hard to believe. Enforcement of the rules that are meant to prevail in the oceans has proved wanting almost everywhere. Even in some of the best-governed democracies, experts admit that overfishing is out of control."

[v] Several other artists have also created indelible images – in paint, photo and other media – based on current and potential environmental collapse. J.Henry Fair, for example, is a New York photographer specializing in images of environmental degradation.

[vi] In one of several related examples, the Cape Farewell project has, since 2002, been taking renowned artists and writers to the High Arctic to inspire them to create works related to climate change. An exhibition of these works was staged at the Natural History Museum in London (UK) in 2006. Under the banner, The Ship, the exhibition celebrated the vessel that carried the artists north, but is also spoke symbolically to the journey that humankind is undertaking. The novelist, Ian McEwan, in an essay introducing the exhibition, aptly framed the question that looms on our real and metaphorical horizon: "How can we begin to restrain ourselves? We resemble a successful lichen, a ravaging bloom of algae, a mould enveloping a fruit".

[vii] Nearly six years on, the project has yet to be built. In January of 2009, the US Minerals management Service issued a positive environmental report for the project, and a formal approval of the lease for the project could be imminent. Time will tell...

[viii] Many would argue that the roots extend much further back. The earliest recorded story, The Epic of Gilgamesh, commented on the dire social and environmental consequences of forest depletion.

[ix] The doctrine of usefulness prevailed into the early 1960s and was typified by the use of resources to spur economic growth. Janet Foster, in her excellent history of conservation in Canada, *Working for Wildlife* (1998), pointed out that even the creation of Banff National Park in 1887 was done for purely utilitarian reasons. "Parks were to be 'commercial assets', sources of revenue to a government foundering in economic depression and burdened by debt from building the Canadian Pacific Railway." The doctrine of usefulness is also plainly evident in the *Prairie Farm Rehabilitation Act* (1935), the *Dominion-Provincial Conference on Reconstruction* (1945), and the *Maritime Marshland Reclamation Act* (1948). Each of these reflected an earnest belief that the Canadian economy could, or should, be stimulated by the use of its natural resources.

[x] The five-year period between 1968 and 1973 saw the publication of several books that collectively sounded a clarion call for attention to the environmental costs of progress. Notable examples are Paul Ehrlich's *The Population Bomb* (1968), the *Whole Earth Catalogue: Access to Tools* (1968), Barry Commoner's *The Closing Circle* (1971), Victor Papanek's *Design for the Real World* (1971), and E.F. Schumacher's influential *Small is Beautiful* (1973). Pierre Dansereau's CBC Massey Lectures,

broadcast in 1972 and published a year later as *Inscape and Landscape*, should also be mentioned here. The lectures called for nothing less than a paradigm shift in mankind's relationship to the natural world.

[xi] This effort has since resulted in the creation of a company, MetroQuest (www.metroquest.com) that does this work for local and regional governments worldwide.

[xii] See C.S. Holling's paper, "The Renewal, Growth, Birth and Death of Ecological Communities", Whole Earth (Summer).

[xiii] SMUD is also testing hydrogen fuel cell vehicles developed by Ford and Daimler Chrysler to gauge real-world driving experience.

[xiv] Against this backdrop, the Genuine Wealth model developed by Mark Anielski is in the vanguard of contemporary thought on wealth and well being. It uses a comprehensive notion of wealth that includes economic, social, and environmental conditions that collectively contribute to the quality of one's life experience.

[xv] The current global financial crisis has cast the limitations of an economy driven by consumer spending – much of it debt financed – into sharp relief.

[xvi] By 2008 global advertising spending had nearly crested half a trillion dollars annually.

HOMAGE

In the quiet hours when we are alone and there is nobody to tell us what fine fellows we are, we come sometimes upon a moment in which we wonder, not how much money we are earning, not how famous we have become, but what good we are doing.

—A. A. Milne

. . . Our house stood in a glade shaded by Douglas firs, I walked beneath those giants every day, a pilgrim passing beneath the arches of a sacred cathedral. The air thick with the smell of life. And if I stopped for a moment, as she taught me, chose to look closely at a small corner of our garden, something special was revealed to me. The spider collecting his breakfast, rewarded for the cunning ingenuity of his silk; ants carrying stray leaves across a blanket of needles; the towhee and robin jousting for turf. She wanted me to see the miracle in these simple rituals. Later, she would take my hand and steer me toward the beach.

I remember the feeling of sand and grass on my feet, between my toes. And then the rush of air as we crested the dunes. I never struggled to break free and run. Even then, especially then, I was awed by nature. And needed to be still, to be humble. How far had these waves traveled, and what had they carried to my beach? What stories, written only for me, were waiting there?

My memories are my talisman.

She was a city girl who came late to country life. But she embraced it, loved it, and shared her love of it with me.

Turning over stones to see what lived underneath, poking the kelp that washed ashore, looking for seals or otters near shore, cupping a mug of hot cocoa. This was my early childhood routine – and it was, I now realize, anything but routine. All children should be so lucky. We probably didn't spend as much time at the beach, or even outside, as I romantically imagine, but there is potency, a resonance in these memories that I carry still. I had books, abundant play, and these forays to the beach. Before my head could get in the way, something took root in my heart. I was learning to care about something, to love something...

ALDO LEOPOLD

Like the man whose words inspired this collection of writings, Aldo Leopold was a key player in the birth of the modern environmental movement in America . The Leopold Wilderness and Gila National Forest are, in fact, often considered the starting point for the wilderness-conservation movement. Susan Flader and Baird Callicott, in the preface to *The River of the Mother of God*, argue, not unconvincingly, that Leopold's *A Sand County Almanac* (1949) surpasses such iconic titles as *Silent Spring*, *Quiet Crisis*, and *The Closing Circle* as the touchstone of the modern environmental movement[ii]. Yes. Leopold's most important work leaves an indelible imprint in the mind. Not least because of his elegant insistence that obligations have no meaning without conscience. And the problem we face as a global community is the extension of social conscience from people to the land.

Leopold understood that you must care about something before you save it – or try to save it. He also expressed this understanding in print at a time when the doctrine of usefulness was still prevalent in "resource management" circles[iii]:

> Conservation is getting nowhere because it is incompatible with our Abrahamic concept of land. We abuse land because we regard it as a commodity belonging to us. When we see land as a community to which we belong, we may begin to use it with love and respect. There is no other way for land to survive the impact of mechanized man, nor for us to reap from it the esthetic harvest it is capable, under science, of contributing to culture.

Leopold wrote those words in 1948, in his forward to *A Sand County Almanac*. The book describes the lands around Leopold's home in Sauk County, Wisconsin, but it is so much more that that. Consisting of three parts (A Sand County Almanac; Sketches Here and There; and

The Upshot), it firstly offers a very personal and intimate chronicle of one year at the Leopold family cottage, dubbed "the shack":

> On this sand farm in Wisconsin, first worn out and then abandoned by our bigger-and-better society, we try to rebuild, with shovel and axe, what we are losing elsewhere. It is here that we seek – and still find – our meat from God.

The folksy tone of these initial pieces, which nonetheless contain an exquisite environmental education in their own right, give way to a more elegiac expression in *Sketches Here and There*. Consider, for example, Leopold's rumination on the crane in "Marshland Elegy":

> Our ability to perceive quality in nature begins, as in art, with the pretty. It expands through successive stages of the beautiful to values as yet uncaptured by language. The quality of cranes lies, I think, in this higher gamut, as yet beyond the reach of words.
>
> This much, though, can be said: our appreciation of the crane grows with the slow unraveling of earthly history. His tribe, we now know, stems out of the remote Eocene. The other members of the fauna in which he originated are long since entombed within the hills. When we hear his call we hear no mere bird. We hear the trumpet in the orchestra of evolution. He is the symbol of our untamable past, of that incredible sweep of millennia which underlies and conditions the daily affairs of birds and men.

And in "Thinking Like a Mountain", Leopold talks passionately about the relationship between wolves, men and mountains – which is, of course, a deeper meditation on the relationship between humans and the environment:

> Only the mountain has lived long enough to listen objectively to the howl of a wolf.
>
> Those unable to decipher the hidden meaning know nevertheless that it is there, for it is felt in all wolf country, and

> distinguishes that country from all other land.
>
> The cowman who cleans his range of wolves does not realize that he is taking over the wolf's job of trimming the herd to fit the range. He has not learned to think like a mountain. Hence we have dustbowls, and rivers washing the future into the sea.
>
> Perhaps this is behind Thoreau's dictum: In wildness is the salvation of the world. Perhaps this is the hidden meaning of the howl of the wolf, long known among mountains, but seldom perceived among men.

It is to Leopold's credit that he wrote those words after beginning this essay with the admission that he had killed a wolf:

> In a second we were pumping lead into the pack...We reached the old wolf in time to watch a fierce green fire dying in her eyes. I realized then, and have known ever since, that there was something new to me in those eyes – something known only to her and to the mountain.

The expression "thinking like a mountain" has become something of a mantra for the environmental, and more recently, sustainability community – and justly so. It is a reminder to see and understand the relationship between seemingly disparate parts of the biotic community as a complete system. Disturbances to one part of the system will have a cascading or ripple effect across the entire system.

In *The Upshot*, Leopold draws his argument to an elegant close with a pointed articulation of his views on the conservation esthetic, wildlife in American culture, wilderness, and the land ethic. While the entire book is an intellectual jewel, this last section is a masterful declaration of Leopold's thoughts on how we might wrest a truly sustainable society from the jaws of progress:

> All ethics so far evolved rest upon a single premise: that the individual is a member of a community of interdependent parts. His instincts prompt him to compete for his place in that community, but his ethics prompt him also to co-operate.

> This sounds simple: do we not already sing our love for and obligation to the land of the free and the home of the brave? Yes, but just what and whom do we love? Certainly not the soil, which we are sending helter-skelter downriver. Certainly not the waters, which we assume have no function except to turn turbines, float barges, and carry off sewage. Certainly not the plants, of which we exterminate whole communities without batting an eye. Certainly not the animals, of which we have already extirpated many of the largest and most beautiful species. A land ethic of course cannot prevent the alteration, management, and use of these 'resources', but it does affirm their right to continued existence, and, at least in spots, their continued existence in a natural state.

The three pillars of thought in *A Sand County Almanac* collectively become the lens through which Leopold develops his land ethic. As he saw it, this was the logical and necessary next step in the evolution of ethics – the expansion of ethics to include non-human members of the biotic community (collectively referred to as "the land"):

> A thing is right when it tends to preserve the integrity, stability, and beauty of the biotic community. It is wrong when it tends otherwise.

A land ethic changes the role of humans from conqueror of the land community to members and citizens of it[iv]

> In human history, we have learned (I hope) that the conqueror role is eventually self-defeating. Why? Because it is implicit in such a role that the conqueror knows, ex cathedra, just what makes the community clock tick, and just what and who is valuable, and what and who is worthless, in community life. It always turns out that he knows neither, and this is why his conquests eventually defeat themselves[v].

I still find it remarkable that Leopold could see with such clarity the path human society should be taking, and transmit that vision to the page so magnificently – long years before the environmental "movement" would gain a footing in 20th century American culture. I also appreciate that Leopold's wisdom was the product of both formal education and real lived experience on the land. Most of all, I celebrate his willingness – perhaps it was more than that, need or his own sense of noblesse oblige – to convey his love of nature, as one who knew all too well that he was part of nature.

As the scholar and conservationist, George Schaller puts it, in a comment worthy of Leopold:

> It is tremendously worrisome that we don't talk about nature anymore. We talk about natural resources as if everything had a price tag...You can't buy spiritual values at a shopping mall. The things that uplift the spirit – an old growth forest, a clear river, the flight of a golden eagle, the howl of a wolf, space and quiet without motors – are intangibles. No one who looks into a gorilla's eyes can remain unchanged...We know that the gorilla still lives within us.

Amen. As we drift ever closer to the centenary of the publication of *A Sand County Almanac*, we would do well to reacquaint ourselves with this work and its author. Leopold was many things: forester, scientist, skilled administrator, and good neighbor – he died of a heart attack while helping his neighbors fight a grass fire – but he was perhaps above all a wonderful writer who saw the future and gave us the means for a course correction:

> But wherever the truth may lie, this much is crystal clear: our bigger-and-better society is now like a hypochondriac, so obsessed with its own economic health as to have lost the capacity to remain healthy. The whole world is so greedy for more bathtubs that it has lost the stability necessary to build them, or even to turn off the tap. Nothing could be more salutary at this stage than a little healthy contempt for a plethora of material blessings.

Read him and be ennobled. Make shift with things as they are.

Essential Reading:

Leopold, A. *A Sand County Almanac*. New York: Oxford University Press, 1949.

Leopold, A. *The River of the Mother of God and Other Essays*. S. L. Flader and J. B. Callicott (eds.), Madison: The University of Wisconsin Press, 1991.

Loren Eiseley

Imagine a high-school drop out and hobo who became the most honored member of the University of Pennsylvania since Benjamin Franklin and you have the provocative "hook" on which to hang a story of Loren Eiseley – anthropologist, science writer, ecologist, poet.

I would love to claim that, as an aspiring writer and student of the environment, my teachers and mentors introduced me to Eiseley. Sadly, that is not how it happened. It was in a used bookstore on Mayne Island, one of the southern gulf islands in British Columbia, Canada. I picked up a slim volume with the intriguing title, *The Immense Journey*. Flipping the book open, I read the following and was beguiled:

> If there is magic on this planet it is contained in water.

There was something in that sentence, perhaps it was the word magic that seemed exactly right. After all, our home is a blue orb in the cosmos; most of our planet is water. As I simply held the idea of "magic" and "water", and opened my mind to other possibilities, two images twisted like fish and then rested for a moment, just long enough for me to catch them, and smile. The first was a summer ritual – camping in the headwaters of the Oyster River – and the sounds of my family as we played, like so many other families across the world, in the water. The second image comes from a much older source and, not being trained as an anthropologist, I can only offer that the image had an emotional or visceral – and not intellectual – resonance. It was the sense of connection with our distant ancestors who crawled out of the water and began the grand experiment of living on land. And so you can imagine my delight when I dipped again into Eiseley:

> The door to the past is a strange door. It swings open and things pass through it, but they pass in one direction only. No man can return across that threshold, though he can look down still and see the green light waver in the waterweeds.

From that moment I knew that I had found a spirit guide to help steer me on my journey – personal, professional, spiritual.

I soon discovered that Eiseley was well known, revered even, for his writings about humanity's relationship to the natural world. His ability to craft a message made him, to my mind anyway, a natural heir to Leopold – both in the transparent poetry of his language and, equally, the potent message about the human imprint, as this excerpt from his essay, "The Angry Winter" makes clear:

> We have become planet changers and the decimators of life, including our own. The sorcerer's gift of fire in a dark cave has brought us more than a simple kingdom. Like so many magical gifts it has conjured up that which cannot be subdued but henceforth demands unceasing attention lest it destroy us.

If Eiseley did no more than frame the human-environment relationship in such gorgeous prose, he would be worth reading, but he did a good deal more. He effortlessly held his science in one hand, while reaching out with the other for the personal, human connection that ultimately lies at the heart of all our stories. Consider this passage from "The Unexpected Universe":

> The archaeologist is the last grubber among things mortal. He puts not men, but civilizations, to bed, and passes upon them final judgments. He finds, if imprinted upon clay, both our grocery bills and the hymns to our gods. Or he uncovers, as I once did in a mountain cavern, the skeleton of a cradled child, supplied, in the pathos of our mortality, with the carefully "killed" tools whose shadowy counterparts were intended to serve a tiny infant through the vicissitudes it would encounter beyond the dark curtain of death. Infinite care had been lavished upon objects that did not equate with the child's ability to use them in this life. Was his spirit expected to grow to manhood, or had this final projection of bereaved parental care thrust into the night, in desperate anxiety, all that an impoverished and simple culture could provide where human affection could not follow?

Eiseley did not pretend to have the answer to what is ultimately an unanswerable query, but in his humanism and poetry he goes a long way to helping us see and appreciate the deeper mystery that is life. Facts and figures have their place, and Eiseley was a distinguished scientist who knew how (and when) to count or measure, but his greater wisdom, I think, came from his ability to admit that science could never answer all of the mysteries of existence. There is wisdom too, and a delightful, lyrical lightness of spirit in his observations of a small rain pool near his office. While most of us might be blind to such a little thing, Eiseley sees the whole of the human experience:

> A few days ago I chanced to look into a rain pool on the walk outside my window. For a long time, because I was dreaming of other things, I saw only the occasional spreading ripple from a raindrop or the simultaneous overlapping circles as the rain fell faster. Then as the beauty and the strange rhythm of the extending and concentric wavelets entered my mind, I saw that I was looking symbolically upon the whole history of our life upon our globe.

And so the magic in water is reaffirmed.

In "The Star Thrower", one of his most famous essays, Eiseley described the experience of being near the beaches of Costabel, and watching what he called the vulturine activity of shell collectors in the pre-dawn hours:

> One can see, in the hour before dawn on the ebb tide, electric torches bobbing like fireflies along the beach. It is the sign of the professional shellers seeking to outrun and anticipate their less aggressive neighbors. A kind of greedy madness sweeps over the competing collectors. After a storm one can see them hurrying along with bundles of gathered starfish, or toppling and overburdened, clutching bags of living shells whose hidden occupants will be slowly cooked and dissolved in the outdoor kettles provided by the resort hotels for the cleaning of specimens.

The counterpoint of this gruesome practice is the star thrower of the title, a solitary man who rescues starfish from the stifling mud and gently throws them back to sea. He collects, but unlike the professional shellers, his interest is in the living:

> "The stars", he said, "throw well. One can help them."
>
> I turned as I neared a bend in the coast and saw him toss another star, skimming it skillfully far out over the ravening and tumultuous water. For a moment, in the changing light, the sower appeared magnified, as though casting larger stars upon some greater sea. He had, at any rate, the posture of a god.

As he returns to his room, Eiseley looks "full at the steaming kettles in which beautiful voiceless things were being boiled alive" and decides to make shift with things as they are.

On a point of land, as though projecting into a domain beyond us, I found the star thrower. In the sweet rain-swept morning, that great many-hued rainbow still lurked and wavered tentatively beyond him. Silently I sought and picked up a still-living star, spinning it far out into the waves. I spoke once briefly. "I understand," I said. "Call me another thrower." Only then I allowed myself to think, He is not alone any longer. After us there will be others.

It may seem a small thing, saving a few sea stars, but I don't think so. It is an act of grace, an act of compassion. It is also an acknowledgement that in saving a piece of nature, no matter how "small", we are saving a part of ourselves.

Loren Eiseley's headstone in West Larel Hill Cemetery in Bala Cynwyd, Pensylvania bears the inscription, "We loved the earth but could not stay". Oh, but he has stayed, and we are the beneficiaries. His words live on and inspire us to reach for our better selves.

Essential Reading:

Eiseley, L. *The Immense Journey*. New York: Random House, 1957.

Eiseley, L. *Darwin's Century*. New York: Doubleday, 1958.

Eiseley, L. *The Firmament of Time*. New York: Atheneum, 1960.

Eiseley, L. *All the Strange Hours: The Excavation of a Life*. New York: Scribner, 1975.

Eiseley, L. *The Star Thrower*. New York: Times Books, 1978.

Peter Drucker[1]

In the month since his death, the requisite accolades have been pouring in for Peter Drucker, the seminal management thinker of the past century. On the face of it then, there would appear to be little to be gained from another tribute – a lone voice that might be lost against an impressively large chorus of admirers and supporters. That said, I am compelled to write because no one has yet pointed out that Drucker made prescient observations about the responsibility of business to society long before the term "sustainability" came into vogue. With his death, the world lost a legitimate "elder", and I was reminded, again, that those of us with an interest in a more just, humane and caring world would do well to read his good words. As early as 1942, for example, he argued that businesses should define "an organizational purpose that goes beyond next-quarter financial results and beyond maximization of shareholder wealth...a purpose that employees can believe in and challenges them to contribute their best work". I revere Drucker because he was a keen observer not of the ball, but the game – he knew in a way that few do that what really matters is the flow of a society through time. Insofar as business is concerned, he knew that the creation of a customer was the only valid definition of business purpose, but the way(s) in which that customer was "created" and continually satisfied mattered a great deal:

> This new concept of social responsibility no longer asks what the limitations on business are, or what business should be doing for those under its immediate authority. It demands that business take responsibility for social problems, social issues, social and political goals and that it become the keeper of society's conscience and the solver of society's problems.?

---

[1] I first wrote this appreciation in 2004. I have revised and extended it for this publication.

In this regard, Drucker anticipated much of what is popularly called corporate social responsibility. He also correctly anticipated the rise of intangible assets as the ultimate sources of wealth creation, writ large, in society. Drucker believed that highly skilled people are an organization's most valuable resource and that a manager's job is to prepare and free people to perform – to recognize the skills in his or her team and create the conditions where those skills are most effectively deployed.

One of the most striking features of what I will call the sustainability "debate" is the failure to draw on the mainstream management and strategy literature in helping to frame both the challenge and opportunity of sustainability. Several recent books have tried to do this, but for the most part, they have not tapped into this influential body of knowledge. More to the point, it is a pity that so few sustainability advocates are familiar with Drucker. We live in an era when business, or as Drucker would prefer, the corporation, is the most influential organization on the planet. It follows that if society is to shift to a more sustainable trajectory, the corporation must play a lead role. To get there, more of us need to know something about how the corporation really works. There are few better places to begin than *Concept of the Corporation.* First published in 1946, this book was the first attempt to show how an organization really worked. Its success established management as a legitimate discipline and field of study. More recently, Management: *Tasks, Responsibilities, Practices*, published in 1973, has long been on my short-list of essential "sustainability" reads. The chapters on management as innovation, and the responsibility of business to society, are clear-eyed accounts of what we need to do to create better corporations, why we need to do it, and most crucially, how we can get on with the job.

Peter Drucker shaped much of my thinking on the nature of the corporation. I owe him an enormous intellectual debt. – a debt that I will enjoy repaying by sharing his insights with others, and using his guidance to help build a more just, humane and caring world.

Essential Reading:

Drucker, P. *Management: Tasks*, Responsibilities, Practices. New York: Harper & Row, Publishers. 1973.

Drucker, P. *Concept of the Corporation*. New Brunswick, NJ: Transaction Publishers. 1993.

Charles David Keeling[2]

On June 16,2005, I wrote about oil cresting $58 a barrel and argued that perhaps the silver lining to rising crude prices was the spur it should provide for investments in alternatives that don't shred the Earth's life support services. Four days later, the world lost a genuine visionary, and the man most responsible for drawing our attention to the buildup of greenhouse gases (GHG) in the atmosphere, with the death of Charles Keeling. He was the world's leading authority on atmospheric GHG accumulation and climate science pioneer at Scripps Institution of Oceanography, University of California, San Diego (UCSD)[vi].

Beginning forty years ago, when the industrial world was basking in the glow of a post-World War II building boom and cars were celebrated signs of progress, Keeling lugged a CO2 monitor to the top of Mauna Loa in Hawaii and began taking the full measure of our "progress". His findings, made famous in the "Keeling Curve" reproduced below as figure 1, demonstrated that CO2 concentrations in the atmosphere were steadily rising – by about 3% a year. The graph has become one of the most famous in science, and a potent symbol of our times.

The Keeling Curve of Atmospheric CO2 Concentration

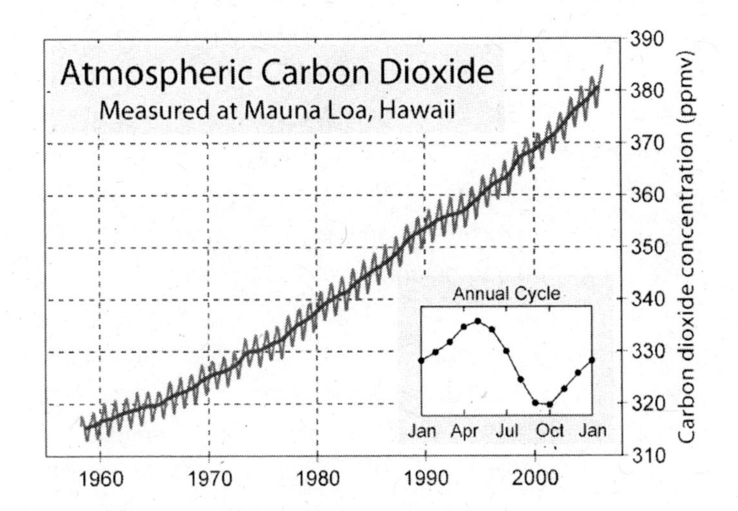

When Keeling began his work, most scientists didn't think that emissions from cars and factories could have a measurable or material effect on the earth's climate, assuming that the CO2 would be absorbed by plants or the oceans. Today, the Keeling Curve is considered the foundation document of global warming research. Charles Kennel, director of the Scripps Institution of Oceanography in San Diego where Keeling worked, has called the data that underpin the Curve "the single most important environmental data set taken in the 20th century". In fact, he has gone so far as to characterize it as one of the three most significant cases of scientific measurement in history:

> There are three occasions when dedication to scientific measurements has changed all of science. Tycho Brahe's observations of planets laid the foundation for Sir Isaac Newton's theory of gravitation. Albert Michelson's measurements of the speed of light laid the foundation for Albert Einstein's theory of relativity. Charles David Keeling's measurements of the global accumulation of carbon dioxide in the atmosphere set the stage for today's profound concerns about climate change.

Today, the majority of climatologists globally agree that increasing levels of CO2 in the atmosphere contribute to ozone depletion, glacial meltdown, and desertification of farmland, among other environmental crimes. Eleven science academies, including the National Academy of Science in the U.S., cited Keeling's work earlier this month when they called on world leaders to acknowledge that the threat of climate change is real and increasing and needs to be addressed. The scale of what needs to be done is not to be taken lightly. James Hansen, NASA's chief climatologist, has stated that the current global CO2 levels of 387 parts per million (ppm) need to be reduced to 350 ppm to preserve the conditions to which life on Earth is adapted. As Thomas Homer Dixon and David Keith have recently pointed out, this kind of global reduction requires substantive change in our energy system:

> Even holding greenhouse gas emissions in the atmosphere to double their pre-industrial level – a limit that still risks severe climate disruption – will require reducing worldwide emissions about 80% below their business-as-usual level by 2050. Such a huge cut, even over 40 years, will require a staggering transformation of the global system.

W.H. Auden once said that a culture is no better than its woods. What he meant was that woodland can be exploited wisely – there is no need for complete preservation, but the unfortunate tendency is for humans to harvest all trees within reach and expand farms onto fragile hillsides, causing drought, flooding and erosion. In a similar way, the burning of small amounts of fossil fuels is one thing, but the creation of an entire economy, indeed an entire world culture, that is hydrocarbon based is quite another. It's been quite a ride, but at what cost? Put another way, is our reliance on fossil fuels what Ronald Wright would call a progress trap? Seems like a good thing in the beginning, but by the time we recognize there may be a problem it's too late to reverse the damage.

Earlier this week, the Senate in the U.S. approved an energy bill that pays lip service to conservation and the legacy of Charles Keeling. The bill calls for utilities to produce 10% of their electricity from renewable sources of energy, and provides tax incentives for people to purchase hybrid cars and energy efficient homes and appliances. These are good things to do, but they fall well short of the catalytic change that is needed to get us off our fossil fuel addiction. And of course, the bill, which must navigate the rough political waters of the House, is silent on drilling for oil in the Alaska Wildlife Refuge, and the need for automakers to get serious about making fuel-efficient cars. Jason Gardner, in his eloquent introduction to The Sacred Earth: Writers on Nature & Spirit, zeroes in on the problem with this type of political action:

> As long as we view the soil, water, plants, and animals through an economic lens, as jobs, or resources for consumption, and not as essential parts of what makes us whole, we will ultimately fail to understand our right and

> responsibility: to extend our concern for ourselves into a concern for everything, and to dispense with the notion that saving the natural world somehow compromises our interests.

We can honor Keeling in at least two ways. First, by grounding our discussions of climate change and the greenhouse effect in good data. Second, by taking real action in the face of incontrovertible evidence – forty years' worth – that our fossil-fuel driven progress just may be the ultimate progress trap.

Essential Reading:

Keeling, C.D. and Pales, J. C. Mauna Loa Carbon Dioxide Project, Report No. 3, pp. 183, 1965.

Revelle, R., chairman: W. Broecker, H. Craig, C. D. Keeling, and J. Smagorinsky, Atmospheric Carbon Dioxide, Report of the Environmental Pollution Panel President's Advisory Committee, The White House, November 1965, 111-133, 1965.

Keeling, C.D. and Bacastow, R. B. Impact of Industrial Gases on Climate, Energy and Climate, Report of Panel on Energy and Climate, R. Revelle, Chairman, National Academy of Sciences, Washington, D. C., 72-95, 1977.

Keeling, C.D. The Influence of Mauna Loa Observatory on the Development of Atmospheric CO2 Research, in *Mauna Loa Observatory 20th Anniversary Report*, edited by J. Miller, National Oceanographic and Atmospheric Administration, Special Report, pp. 36-54, 1978.

HERMAN DALY

In October of 2003 I made a pilgrimage from my home on Canada's west coast to the Fairmont Jasper Park Lodge in Jasper National Park, Alberta. The official occasion was the Canadian Society for Ecological Economics international meeting. The unofficial occasion, and the reason for my attendance, was to pay homage to Herman Daly, one of the true elders, in the broadest and best sense of that term, in the sustainability community and one of the sanest voices calling for a dramatic reordering of the way our economy works. Lest there be any doubt, I believe Daly should win a Nobel Prize – the economics prize would seem to be obvious, but he is also justly deserving of the peace prize – but, having met the man, I know he isn't motivated by such trappings. All the more reason we should venerate him.

In 1973, the date seems incredible to me now, Daly edited a pathbreaking book, *Toward a Steady-State Economy*. In it, he and a courageous group of scholars[viii] unfolded an elegant map to "revise our economic thinking so that it will be more in conformity with the finite energy and resource limits of the earth". In this regard, Daly *et al* proved themselves worthy bearers of the torch previously carried by Leopold. I didn't get a chance to ask Daly directly, but I bet he well knew that Leopold was motivated by the question of "whether a still higher 'standard of living' is worth its cost in things natural, wild and free".

I refer to the 1973 publication to underscore the fact that for more than three decades Daly has been asking fundamental questions about the size of the economy relative to the ecosystem, as well as questions about allocative efficiency[ix] and distributive justice[x] – questions that challenge the received wisdom of economics[xi]. This is lonely work because it challenges the status quo, and not just at the margins, but much closer to the core. And it is shameful that so few "mainstream" economists have accepted the inevitability of Daly's argument – it is, indeed, a defining example of the idea whose time has come. And so I believe we will eventually see an overthrow of the economic establishment, and we will begin to treat the environmental and social costs of production as something more than "externalities"[xii]. The question is how much will we have lost while waiting for the economic scales to tip in Daly's (and our) favor?

The foundation of Daly's work is a steadfast belief that the economy must be viewed as a subsystem of the containing ecosystem, and as such, unrestricted economic growth is something be avoided:

> The power of the concept of sustainable development is that it both reflects and evokes a latent shift in our vision of how the economic activities of human beings are related to the natural world – an ecosystem which is finite, non-growing, and materially closed. The demands of these activities on the containing ecosystem for regeneration of raw material "inputs" and absorption of waste "outputs" must, I will argue, be kept at ecologically sustainable levels as a condition of sustainable development.

Daly has taken economics into new territory by arguing that growth is not necessarily the right measure of social welfare[xiii], and more to the point, that growth and development should not be confused. "When something grows it gets bigger, when something develops it gets different". The economy must eventually stop growing, but it can continue to develop by shifting to conceptions of wealth that are defined not be conventional metrics such as gross national product, but by a throughput of matter-energy that is within the regenerative and assimilative capacities of the ecosystem.

Steven Stoll, in his delightful book, *The Great Delusion*, paints a rather graphic picture of the current fixation on economic "growth":

> There are certain places where the scope and scale of economic growth come into view, where I stop, as though gazing over the Grand Canyon, and just wonder. One of those places is Costco. It begins with shopping carts broad enough to seat two children side by side. The carts had better be big. They need to haul one-gallon jars of mayonnaise, 117-ounce cans of baked beans, 340-ounce jugs of liquid detergent, and 70-ounce boxes of breakfast cereal. The coolers advertised for

> summer picnics hold 266 cans. Giant warehouse stores, shelved to the ceiling with goods from all the waters and forests of the world, make no excuses for consumption...The question that comes to my mind whenever I catch a glimpse of aggregate consumption is always the same: How can it last?
>
> The answer, of course, is that it can't. As Daly would put it:
>
> Current economic growth has uncoupled itself from the world and has become irrelevant. Worse, it has become a blind guide.

Herman Daly is sounding an important note within economics, and the sustainability community, by challenging the so-called "canonical assumption" of economics, namely, that growth is good. He is trying to expand and improve economic theory by not limiting analysis to the circular flow of exchange value (firms to households), but adding the one-way throughput of matter and energy because it is this throughput that ties human society to the environment. Every production and consumption decision, by businesses, by individual households, by governments, must be made with the understanding that there are natural capital depletion and pollution consequences. The scale of the economic system within which these decisions take place therefore matters a great deal. Is the total amount of production in the economy and the resource depletion and pollution that results – is this scale within the absorptive and regenerative capacity of the ecosystem? Or are we destroying natural capital too quickly for our own good? The welfare effects of destroying natural capital may be greater than the welfare benefits of what has been produced and consumed.

The evidence continues to mount that our ecosystem, upon which all economic (and other) wealth ultimately depends, is in retreat. Herman Daly has a good idea to help reform the way we think about and measure progress. Sadly, it is a truism that we don't give credit to the first person to have an idea, but to the first to take it seriously. Accordingly, read Daly and join the expanding pool of "ecological economists". The hour is late and we need to find someone to take his idea seriously.

Essential Reading:

Daly, H. and Cobb, Jr., J.B. *For the Common Good: Redirecting the Economy toward Community, the Environment, and a Sustainable Future*, 2nd ed. Boston: Beacon Press, 1994.

Daly, H. Beyond Growth: *The Economics of Sustainable Development*. Boston, Beacon Press, 1996.

Daly, H., ed. *Toward a Steady-State Economy*. San Francisco: W.H. Freeman and Co., 1973

The Passing of a Holy Trinity: Time for a New Generation to Carry the Torch[3]

The closing verse of "In Flanders Fields" begins with a lyrical invocation: "Take up our quarrel with the foe: To you from failing hands we throw the torch; be yours to hold it high". While John McCrae, the Canadian physician who penned those great words, was concerned with the plight of young men and women who gave their lives for their country, his call should also remind us to honor those who came before in all aspects of human endeavor, and to carry the metaphorical torch on the next stage of its journey. I've thought of this a good deal recently as three of North America's leading public intellectuals have passed from the stage. Within a span of less than 3 weeks in April of 2006, William Sloane Coffin, Jane Jacobs, and John Kenneth Galbraith died. And with their passing the world lost an irretrievable part of its intellectual legacy. It now falls to a younger generation to step up and lead our society. I wonder if we are up to it?

The Rev. William Sloane Coffin Jr. was a liberal Christian clergyman, but he was so much more than that. A ridiculously talented man, Coffin was a superb athlete, an accomplished pianist, a CIA agent, and later, the chaplain of Yale University and a leader in the civil-rights and peace movements of the 1960s and 1970s. He opposed United States military intervention from Vietnam to Iraq and wasn't afraid to use his pulpit as a platform for like-minded crusaders, notably Martin Luther King Jr., Desmond Tutu and Nelson Mandela. Coffin was also the inspiration for the character Rev. Sloan in the Doonesbury comic strip.

Coffin understood that real courage wasn't about never being afraid; rather, it was about doing the right thing despite being afraid. Nowhere was this more evident than in his commentary on American foreign policy and the need to distinguish patriotism from nationalism:

> Patriotism at the expense of another nation is as wicked as racism at the expense of another race. Let us resolve to be patriots always,

[3] First written and posted online (www.abbottstrategies.com) in 2006. Revised for this publication.

> nationalists never. Let us love our country, but pledge allegiance to the earth and to the flora and fauna and human life that it supports — one planet indivisible, with clean air, soil and water; with liberty, justice and peace for all.

In the introduction to Coffin's exemplary collection of quotations, *Credo*, James Carroll recalls the night in 1972 when he and Coffin and numerous other ministers were thrown in jail for trespassing at the U.S. Capitol while protesting the war in Vietnam. Despite no doubt feeling some degree of fear, Coffin's booming baritone voice broke the jailhouse silence, as he sung Handel's "Messiah" and in doing so, comforted the frightened men of the cloth.

As with all of the individuals I pay homage to in this section of the book, Coffin was far ahead of his time in seeing what needed to be done to make the world a kinder, more humane place. He saw three specific causes that needed urgent attention – disarmament, the environment, and the gap between the rich and poor of the world. With respect to disarmament, he served as president of the SANE/FREEZE campaign for global security, the largest peace and justice organization in the United States that specifically called for disarmament and a freeze on nuclear testing.. On the environment, Coffin's views were clear:

> We should be God's stewards of creation, or as the Orthodox say, "We should be priests of God's creation." We need to stop the depletion of the ozone layer and the greenhouse effect.

As for narrowing the gap between rich and poor, Coffin saw a synergistic relationship with environmental stewardship as he opined:

> If Abraham Lincoln was right, that a nation cannot long endure half-slave, half-free, the world is not going to long endure, partly-prosperous, mostly-miserable. We simply have to do something to narrow the chasm between rich and poor here at home and also throughout the whole world.
>
> If we had solar energy, for instance, there would be an unlimited source of benign energy. What that would mean for most of the poor folk in this world who live in the southern

> tier, Central America, Latin America, Africa, Asia! The one thing that they all have in abundance is sunshine. Instead of putting research and development into weapons, put them into renewable energy like that. We would have a world that God could really smile on.

An inspiring speaker, Coffin has been a source of encouragement to me with his reminder that:

> We don't have to be "successful", only valuable. We don't have to make money, only a difference, and particularly in the lives society counts least and puts last.

Jane Jacobs is justly famous for *The Death and Life of Great American Cities*, a book that the New York Times Book Review called "perhaps the most influential work in the history of town planning". And justly so. The book is a brilliant critique of the urban renewal policies of the 1950s, which, Jacobs claimed, destroyed communities and created isolated, unnatural urban spaces. She advocated dense, mixed-use neighborhoods and cited Greenwich Village in New York City as an example of a vibrant urban community. Her razor sharp critique of conventional planning was evident from the introductory pages:

> There is a wistful myth that if only we had enough money to spend – the figure is usually put at a hundred billion dollars – we could wipe out all our slums in ten years, reverse decay in the great, dull, gray belts that were yesterday's and day-before-yesterday's suburbs, anchor the wandering middle class and its wandering tax money, and perhaps even solve the traffic problem.
>
> But look what we have built with the first several billions: Low-income projects that become worse centers of delinquency, vandalism and general social hopelessness than the slums they were supposed to replace. Middle-income housing projects which are truly marvels of dullness and regimentation, sealed against any buoyancy or vitality of city life. Luxury housing projects that mitigate their inanity, or try

> to, with a vapid vulgarity. Cultural centers that are unable to support a good bookstore. Civic centers that are avoided by everyone but bums, who have fewer choices of loitering place than others. Commercial centers that are lackluster imitations of standardized suburban chain-store shopping. Promenades that go from no place to nowhere and have no promenaders. Expressways that eviscerate great cities. This is not the rebuilding of cities. This is the sacking of cities.

Bravo. And yet, while *The Death and Life of American Cities* legitimately turned urban planning on its head, I believe *The Economy of Cities* will continue to grow in stature and may ultimately stand as her most lasting contribution to the intellectual firmament. Here, Jacobs identified the creative milieu of a diverse city as an essential prerequisite for economic growth. This particular work influenced, among others, Nobel Laureate Robert Lucas at the University of Chicago[xiv]. John Barber, writing in *The Globe and Mail*, aptly described the scope of Jacobs' influence:

> When she wasn't destroying the academy of urban planning in a stunning display of the power of ideas, or rewriting world history and macroeconomic theory to reveal the seminal role of cities, she was teaching us how to live in them.

In addition to her potent thinking and writing on the shape of urban spaces, Jacobs was a deft community activist who is well known for organizing grass-roots efforts to block urban-renewal projects that she felt would destroy local neighborhoods. She was instrumental in the eventual cancellation of the Lower Manhatten Expressway, as well as the Spadina Expressway in Toronto.

As a tribute to Jacobs, the Rockefeller Foundation announced on February 9, 2007 the creation of the Jane Jacobs Medal, "to recognize individuals who have made a significant contribution to thinking about urban design, specifically in New York City."

John Kenneth Galbraith, the towering (he stood 6'9") Canadian-American economist, diplomat, and raconteur, became famous in

1958 with the publication of *The Affluent Society*, but there was more to his life and career than this iconic title. In addition to his long tenure at Harvard, and wartime (WWII) experience in the Office of Price Administration, Galbraith served in the administrations of four US Presidents (Franklin D. Roosevelt, Harry S. Truman, John F. Kennedy, and Lyndon B. Johnson), was editor of *Fortune* magazine for several years, director of the US Strategic Bombing Survey, chairman of the Americans for Democratic Action in the late 1960s, and a successful television and newspaper commentator. He also served as the American ambassador to India in the early 1960s and was a critically and commercially successful novelist (A Tenured Professor)

While *The Affluent Society* brought Galbraith fame, it also, as perhaps all influential texts must, brought him criticism from pro-market economists who were offended by his post-materialist message. In the book, Galbraith, echoing Thorsten Veblen[xv], argued that industrial production was being devoted to satisfying trivial consumer needs, in part to maintain employment, and that the United States should shift resources to improve schools, infrastructure, recreational resources, and social services, providing a better quality of life instead of an ever greater quantity of consumer goods. To underscore his point, he noted that while many Americans were able to purchase luxury items, their parks were polluted and their children attended poorly maintained schools. His critique influenced efforts during the 1960s to improve the quality of public institutions and facilities, and is an often-overlooked contribution to the modern environmental movement. More recently, Galbraith's slim volume, *The Good Society: The Humane Agenda*, can now be seen as a prescient comment on several aspects of American policy, notably foreign policy:

> The good society must accept that in the relations between rich countries and poor, between the former colonial powers and their colonies, the world and the human situation have changed for all time. The foreign policy of the good society must still be sensitive to the past and particularly to anything that may seem to suggest a resurgent exercise in colonialism.

> This is especially necessary in the case of the United States. The largest and militarily the most dominant of the former imperial powers or of those so regarded, it naturally arouses the greatest fear of some imperial residuum. This is heightened by the frequent and often ill-considered reference to the need of the United States to exercise leadership in the world community, to assume it natural leadership role. Caution and restraint are here of prime importance. Leadership, initiative, are, of course, still required, but in the modern world they must be a wise and normally a collective response to need, not a seeming manifestation of imperial right.
>
> The fortunate countries must now deal with the imperial legacy – the grave, indeed intolerable, human suffering left in its wake.

If only such wise counsel had been followed before, and especially after, the terrorist attacks in the United States on September 11, 2001.

Collectively, Coffin, Jacobs and Galbraith had the capacity to, as John Ralston Saul would have it, find out what's truly going on in society and talk about it. I would add that they did so with rare panache. And now they are gone. How to fill the void?

Today we bow before the twin altars of abstraction and specialization. And to be sure there are benefits to society of specialist knowledge, but it seems to me that the enduring legacy, and lesson, of Coffin, Jacobs and Galbraith is to keep our perspectives firmly rooted in the reality of how things actually work, and to not lose sight of the public good. Let's not assume anything; instead, let's pay attention to the simple things that often aren't so simple at all. The messy vitality of neighborhood streets that don't all look the same; real-life experiences that trump abstract economic theory, particularly the idea of consumer sovereignty in an age of omnipresent advertising; the virtue of keeping the future open and flexible. Put another way, let's loosen our grip on theory and science just a little and seek a visceral connection with the world, and with the communities of which we are a part.

Finally, and most importantly, let us follow the example of Patagonia founder, Yvon Chouinard, a worthy heir to Coffin *et al*, who once observed that "evil doesn't always have to be an overt act, it can be merely the absence of good". He added that if you have the opportunity and the ability to do good and you choose to do nothing, you are complicit in the creation or perpetuation of evil. I couldn't agree more. In 1986 Chouinard committed his company to "tithing" 1% of sales or 10% of profits, whichever is greater each year to environmental activism. In 1994 he raised the bar yet higher by moving Patagonia to using organic cotton – sparking creation of the organic cotton industry in California. We best fill the void created by the passing of our elders by absorbing their lessons and example, and giving them new life through our voices and our example. Onward.

ESSENTIAL READING:

COFFIN:

Coffin, W.S. *Credo*. New York: Westminster John Knox Press, 2003.

Coffin, W.S. *One to Every Man*. New York: Atheneum, 1977.

JACOBS:

Jacobs, J. *The Death and Life of Great American Cities*. New York: Vintage Books, 1992 (first published in 1961)

Jacobs, J. *The Economy of Cities*

Jacobs, J. *Systems of Survival: A Dialogue on the Moral Foundations of Commerce and Politics*

Jacobs, J. *The Nature of Economies*.

GALBRAITH:

Galbraith, J.K. *The Affluent Society*. Boston: Houghton Mifflin Company, 1958.

Galbraith, J.K. *The New Industrial State*. Princeton, New Jersey: Princeton University Press, 2007.

Galbraith, J.K. *The Good Society: The Humane Agenda*. Boston: Houghton Mifflin Company, 1996.

NOTES TO SECTION 2

[i] As early as 1935, Leopold and others formed the Wilderness Society to protect and preserve America's wild places. The efforts of the Society were instrumental in passage of the Wilderness Act in 1964.

[ii] The New York Public Library, in a wonderful millennial project called "Books of the Century", identified A Sound County Almanac as a defining contribution to our understanding of human-environment interactions.

[iii] My earlier book, *Uncommon Cents: Thoreau and the nature of Business* (Green Frigate Books, 2008) provides additional context and commentary on the roots of the American environmental movement. For example, a century before Leopold, Thoreau had bravely criticized the emerging market economy for its impacts on the environment, and George Perkins Marsh, in his magisterial book, *Man and Nature* (Harvard University Press, 1864), had sounded concern about the human imprint on nature. And of course, the battle between John Muir and Gifford Pinchot over the decision to flood the Hetch Hetchy Valley in the early 20th century is the stuff of environmental management lore. Still, it is, I think, fair to say that Leopold was prescient in his call for a land ethic. As he put it, "We of the minority see a law of diminishing returns in progress; our opponents do not." The current state of our planet's natural capital assets would suggest that Leopold was right; we have had rather too much "progress".

[iv] The reference to citizen here is important; contemporary authors and scholars such as James Howard Kunstler have, I think rightly, pointed out that human society must shift from being "consumers" to "citizens" – with rights to be sure, but equally with obligations to each other.

[v] This theme is elegantly developed in several recent books, notably Ronald Wright's A Short History of Progress (Carroll & Graf, 2004); Jared Diamond's Collapse (Penguin, 2005); and Paul Bahn and John Flenley's Easter Island, Earth Island (Thames and Hudson, 1992).

[vi] Scripps Institution of Oceanography, at UC San Diego, is one of the oldest, largest and most important centers for global science research and education in the world. The National Research Council has ranked Scripps first in faculty quality among oceanography programs nationwide. Now in its second century of discovery, the scientific scope of the institution has grown to include biological, physical, chemical, geological, geophysical and atmospheric studies of the earth as a system. Hundreds of research programs covering a wide range of scientific areas are under way today in 65 countries. The institution has a staff of about 1,300, and annual expenditures of approximately $155 million from federal, state and private sources. Scripps operates one of the largest U.S. academic fleets with four oceanographic research ships and one research platform for worldwide exploration.

[vii] In addition to tracking CO2 in the Earth's atmosphere at the summit of the Mauna Loa volcano in Hawaii, Keeling also collected measurements on CO2 at another of the world's last wildernesses – the South Pole.

[viii] The group of contributors included many of the most luminous names in the environmental, economics, philosophical, and theological firmament, among them Kenneth Boulding, John Cobb, Paul Ehelich, Nicholas Georgescu-Roegen, Garrett Hardin, C.S. Lewis, Donella Meadows, and E.F. Schumacher.

Reflection

The great thing in this world is not so much where we stand, but in which direction we are moving.

—Oliver Wendell Holmes

[ix] One of the historic strengths of economics, which Daly acknowledges and supports, is its attention to decentralized decision-making coordinated by markets and price system – allocative efficiency (the efficient allocation of scarce resources among competing ends).

[x] Distribution is about the way in which resources are shared within society – fundamentally, is the sharing fair?

[xi] Daly's interest in these fundamental questions probably extends further back; in 1967-68 he was a Ford Foundation Visiting Professor at the University of Ceara, Brazil, and it was during this appointment that he began investigating the environmental constraints to economic growth.

[xii] The eminent economist, William Nordhaus, commenting on climate change, elegantly discusses the problem of externalities thusly:
Virtually every activity directly or indirectly involves combustion of fossil fuels, producing emissions of carbon dioxide into the atmosphere. The carbon dioxide accumulates over many decades and leads to surface warming along with many other potentially harmful geophysical changes. Emissions of carbon dioxide represent "externalities", i.e. social consequences not accounted for by the workings of the market. They are market failures because people do not pay for the current and future costs of their actions.

[xiii] It should be noted that Daly is not alone in questioning growth; Marilyn Waring (who studied the UN System of National Accounts), has also posited the idea of uneconomic growth.

[xiv] It should also be noted that popular commentators on the creative forces that underpin cities such as Richard Florida owe a not insignificant intellectual debt to Jane Jacobs – they are popular, but they are not the first to comment on the city in this regard.

[xv] Veblen is best known for his 1899 book, The Theory of the Leisure Class, in which he observes that the rich (and not so rich) try to impress each other through displays of conspicuous consumption (a term he coined), and seek opportunities for conspicuous leisure.

. . . To catch a trout you must know about water. This was his first lesson. Pay attention to where and how it flows, where it pools, where it dances over stones. And so I learned about water.

It began on the Oyster River, a sacred place for him. I remember standing on a rock in bare feet, splaying my toes for purchase on this smooth bone of the Earth. Holding his fly rod, a beautiful piece of split cane that felt alive in my hand, I didn't so much cast as drop the line and fly, a small mosquito, into the thundering foam. The current would do the rest. And it did. Gently stripping line off with my left hand and letting it run out, pulled by the weight of water, I will always remember the electricity in my body at the first tug of a trout.

I got better – never as good as my brothers, who could really think like a fish, but good enough to hold my own. But of course, that wasn't the point. For me, fishing was a meditation. And the opportunity to learn from a master.

His wisdom was won by experience, advancing years. And he was sharing it with me. No greater gift.

We fished early in the morning, and again after dinner. Trying our luck in the good water. Trout, toast and tea by a riverside fire our rich reward.

I remember a summer evening on the Marble River, west of port Hardy on Vancouver Island. The air beginning to cool as the sun slipped low in the sky. We had waded to a small island in the middle of a long, sinuous curve of water. As I prepared to cast he pulled a pouch of tobacco from his vest and began the ritual familiar to all who smoke a pipe. Such a tableaux: a father enjoying the first puffs from a fresh pipe while his youngest son looks for trout in the twilight of a summer eve in a canyon sculpted by water, wind and time. I worked the line out toward a submerged log. When the fish hit we both knew it was a big one. What I remember, what I cherish, are two things: his childlike excitement as I played the fish in close to shore, and the way he waded into the river to make sure this one didn't get away. All without missing a puff on his pipe.

He had emotional balance, even serenity, in the face of existential experiences. Like pain. He had cancer, and was slowly dying.

Why did we fish? To connect with an ancestral spirit certainly, but also to connect with each other. The connection between generations that makes lives complete.

The last time we fished together he was on a break from the chemo, and he walked with me. Reading the water, reading me. I hooked, and lost, a large trout that day. But all he said was "you've mastered all that I know about water".

This is how I remember him…

Sustainability, Leadership and the Need for a Story[1]

One of the more interesting philosophical debates among those with an interest in sustainability pits what I will call the reformers against the revolutionaries. Let me explain. The reformers believe that while there may be a few genuinely bad companies out there, it is absolutely possible to reform the majority and weave sustainability into day-to-day business. The revolutionaries, as the name suggests, are skeptical (or worse) about the corporation and believe we must forge a bold new future with new types of social and commercial enterprise.

I thought of this recently as I read Janet McFarland's useful column in the *Globe and Mail*, "The corporate call for integrity seems little more than lip service". You see, I have long placed myself in the reformer's camp. In fact, I have been quick to defend the majority of corporations and have suggested that the Achilles heel of the sustainability movement is its too frequent insistence on seizing the moral high ground and preaching to the converted. What about the other 80 or 90%? While I'm not yet ready to declare myself a revolutionary, Ms. McFarland's column gave me pause and reminded me that my reformation argument rests on an important assumption about corporate leadership that is too often ignored or overlooked. Put simply, unless and until corporate boards and the CEOs they hire accept responsibility for the behavior of their firms, our ability to institute reforms that foster sustainability will be gravely compromised.

In the lingering fallout from the collapse of Enron, Adelphia, WorldCom and others (will the ripples from this story never cease?); CEO ignorance is becoming a trendy excuse and defense tactic. And so it is that Ken Lay, at once both notorious and pathetic as the fallen chief of Enron, can claim that he knew nothing about the financial transactions and accounting practices that ultimately sunk his company. Further, he can protest that his personal wealth has been "diminished" to some $20 million and that he is therefore also a "victim".

---

[1] First written and posted online (www.abbottstrategies.com) in 2005. Revised and expanded for this publication.

What is going on here? What do such claims of ignorance say about how we should think about and measure CEOs? I respectfully submit that the fundamental measure of a CEO is his or her ability to lead. But what, ultimately does this mean and what is the narrative, the story leaders should craft to galvanize their employees and other stakeholders?

In business, as in so much of life today, we emphasize outcomes in thinking about leadership – increased sales, reduced costs, shareholder value, and so on. We also, it must be said, value power and charisma and associate this with leadership. Our implicit or explicit evaluation of corporate leaders and our apparent willingness to worship at the cult of celebrity leaders (think Donald Trump) only reinforces this view. The methods through which outcomes are achieved, however, has tended to receive rather less attention. In particular, the moral principles that underpin the ideology of leaders are a subject that cries out for discussion and debate.

If we are interested in creating genuine financial and social wealth or well being, if we are interested in sustainability or social responsibility, why wouldn't we see the imperative of exploring the moral dimension of boards and CEOs? As Ms. McFarland aptly put it, morality "is not endlessly flexible". More broadly, Miles Little, Director and Founder of the Centre for Values, Ethics and the Law in Medicine at the University of Sydney, reminds us that merely thinking about leadership in the instrumental sense of being the means through which followers achieve a particular interest (shareholder value comes to mind) is to focus too narrowly on *"the kind of leadership that can have an ideological base without necessarily having a moral one. Leadership without a moral basis is almost always potentially disastrous."*

The news is not all bad. Just as Camus generously and wisely noted that in a time of pestilence there are more things to admire in men than to despise, I passionately believe that there are many more good companies than bad. I further believe that more and more companies and organizations are thinking about the moral dimension of governance. Viewed in this light, sustainability or social responsibility can become an emergent property of doing business or exercising leadership. Canada is especially fortunate in this regard. The most recent KPMG – Ipsos Reid ranking of Canadian corporations noted that the two companies which score highest for corporate governance, RBC Financial Group and BCE Inc., also top the social responsibility rankings. RBC also happens to be Canada's most respected corporation overall.

And what might all of this mean for my ultimate desire of framing sustainability properly? It's about leadership, to be sure, the ability to catalyze individuals to work as a team in pursuit of something bigger than themselves, but it is also more than that. It is about remembering the power of stories.

Robert Altman's wonderfully cynical film about the movie business, *The Player*, contains an essential truth about stories that advocates of sustainability would do well to remember. In the film, the central character is asked why a particular screenplay wasn't filmed. He says it lacked certain qualities necessary to make a commercially successful movie. There is a pause. He expands on his answer. He says up, as opposed to down; happy as opposed to sad; hopeful as opposed to desperate; and a happy ending...especially a happy ending. His point is that while all people like stories; *most* people like stories that offer hope – and a happy ending. Stories in which good triumphs over evil. Stories propelled by an engaging and entertaining narrative – the route to the happy ending matters.

Now consider the way in which the sustainability "story" has been told. Is it any wonder the majority of people have tuned out? So many of the efforts to get more people "living like they plan on staying" read and sound like a mother trying to coax her kids to eat vegetables – this may not taste good, but it's good for you! We can do better. We need to do better.

Lest readers wonder if I've forgotten about those relatively well-known individuals, cities and organizations that are brokering novel collaborations and incubating new sustainable business models and technologies, I'm *not* talking here about the relatively thin edge of real leaders who are blazing a trail in support of a story that is at once uniquely their own and supportive of the communities of which they are a part. Instead, I'm talking about "the other 80%", the large clot of individuals, cities and organizations whose behavior must change if society is ever to approach a relationship with the Earth that can be called sustainable.

The complex patterns of interaction that characterize biological and human systems doubtless cry out for new ideas, technologies and collaborations, but what is most needed is a new story. And that story is not about making people aware of the true costs of energy, to take a topical example, or pointing out that non-carbon alternatives to gasoline are available that won't cramp anyone's style. This is subtext. The real story is about home – the places we live, and our relationships with others. The real story is about how we give meaning and value to the idea of home. Ted Chamberlin makes this point beautifully in his protean book, *If This Is Your Land, Where Are Your Stories?*

> Except for the idea of a creator, there is no idea quite as bewildering as the idea of home, nor one that causes as many conflicts...Can one land ever really be home to more than one people? To native and newcomer, for instance? Or to Arab and Jew, Hutu and Tutsi, Albanian and Kosovar, Turk and Kurd? Can the world ever be home to all of us? I think so. But not until we have reimagined Them and Us.

Throughout history humans have divided the world and its peoples into friend and foe, them and us – with catastrophic results. And we continue to do so today, and not simply at a national or international scale. Look closely at any city, or indeed at any organization, and you will see the separation of people into distinct camps, cliques, or tribes. One of the most important things we lose through this separation is an awareness and appreciation for other people's stories and the lessons they might hold:

> Other people's stories are as varied as the landscapes and languages of the world; and the storytelling traditions to which they belong tell the different truths of religion and science, of history and the arts. They tell people where they came from, and why they are here; how to live, and

> sometimes how to die. They come in many different forms, from creation stories to constitutions, from southern epics and northern sagas to native American tales and African praise songs, and from nursery rhymes and national anthems to myths and mathematics.

So, how to move forward? How to write the kind of story the sustainability cause needs? The answer will not be found in the usual places. Which is to say that benchmarking studies, stakeholder engagement exercises, and business case development – all tools of the trade for most sustainability efforts – must be viewed as accents and nuance. They enrich the narrative, but they are not the narrative. Just as special effects never make up for a lack of plot in a movie. Should we talk to people and create business cases to support an argument for sustainability? Yes, but we should recognize the limits of such an approach. To paraphrase the business strategist, Gary Hamel, customers are notoriously lacking in foresight – they often don't know they want something until it is thrust upon them. We therefore need to forge a story about sustainability that hasn't been told yet (or told well). We need to shape a compelling vision of the future, and sell that vision with the kind of passion, money and marketing savvy that Hollywood sells movies. We need to convince people through the art of storytelling that this vision is worth fighting for. And it's okay if the story seems strange – this is what will first take hold of us (and others) and make us believe it.

Nothing happens without first a dream. My dream is a world in which human society lives in a more sustainable relationship with the Earth, and with each other. To get there, we need leadership, but we also, crucially, need to write a new story – a story about the future and what can be done now to secure it. We also need to sell this story in ways that heretofore have been overlooked by the sustainability community. We have a great cause; what we lack is a story to grow the constituency of supporters for that cause.

Thoughts on the World's Most Admired Companies[2]

Like most people, I find lists seductive because they invariably spur friendly (and sometimes not so friendly) debate. Q magazine's recent list of 100 songs that changed the world is a good example. In a business context, Fortune magazine's annual ranking of America's most admired companies, and the best companies to work for, respectively, are eagerly awaited and sell out within a few days of release. This year, I noted that General Electric, which had topped the most admired list for 5 years, suffered from its embarrassing golden handshake with Jack Welch and dropped to #5, and Wal-Mart topped the most admired list but didn't even make it onto the list of the 100 best companies to work for. And therein lies something exciting – the emergence of a new business ethos. Let me explain.

Much has been written of late, and doubtless more said, about sustainability, the interplay of economic, social and environmental aspirations. In fact, it's become *de rigueur* for business and government leaders, the NGO community, and their advisors, to talk about the importance or "value" of sustainability. I'm culpable here; I've argued for some time that sustainability should be dragged out of the middle management trenches and placed squarely on the CEO's agenda. And so it is that I compared the two Fortune lists to see if there was any overlap. If I was right that what we call sustainability should inform the strategy process, then the companies we most admire should, among other things, be great places to work.

The results initially surprised, and discouraged me. Just as Wal-Mart topped one list but didn't make the other, Edward Jones, the best company to work for, didn't crack the most admired list. But as I looked a little deeper I began to see more overlap. Microsoft, #7 on the most admired list, was #20 on the best to work for scale, and Starbucks, #9 on the most admired list, came in at #47. In all, 37 of the 100 best companies to work for also made the most admired list.

[2] First written and posted online in 2003. Revised and expanded for this publication.

What should we read into these results? First, careful readers of the *Fortune* rankings will point out that the methodology used to compile the two lists differs and that any comparative results should be interpreted with caution. Fair enough. But I think we're beginning to see a broadening or maturing of business strategy to include many of the principles of sustainability. Make no mistake, there's still much to learn and even more to do, but smart companies realize that attracting bright people and keeping them motivated and excited is a recipe for success. Some might call this paying attention to the social bottom line, but I prefer to see it as an exciting evolution of the competitive strategy process. Closer to home, the top three points of differentiation on *BC Business*' ranking of the province's most respected companies last year were customer service, treatment of employees, and environmental performance. Not a bad proxy for sustainability, and not a bad basis for describing how your firm will compete.

There are those who might argue that any ranking of companies from any business magazine is suspect, and that my attempt to draw a link with sustainability is apocryphal. To them I would point out that Business Ethics' annual ranking of the 100 best corporate citizens in America has just been released, and 3 of the top 5 can also be found on Fortune's list of the 50 most admired companies in the world. In fact, 5 of the top 10 companies on the global 50 are on the Business Ethics' list. These companies – Microsoft, Dell, Procter & Gamble, IBM and FedEx might be thought of as old dogs (they've all been around for at least 2 decades), but it is perhaps more useful to see them as grey-haired revolutionaries, to use Gary Hamel's term. They aren't afraid to raise the height of their radar, listen to the winds of change, and adjust their strategic position. Put another way, they aren't afraid to learn new tricks. The ability to see the relationship between shareholder results and broad social and environmental concerns may be the greatest trick of all. I believe we'll see more companies follow suit in the years to come.

In Defense of the Corporation

In a 1998 executive briefing at Stanford University, Gary Hamel, the noted strategist and author, said that if you wanted to create shareholder value, you hired a 60-year old CEO, gave him a boatload of shares, imposed a mandatory retirement age of 62, and got out of the way.

He wisely added that whether the almost inevitable bump in share price created genuine wealth was an open question. I was reminded of this anecdote as I watched a popular documentary film currently making the rounds called *The Corporation*. In Canada, it has quickly become the most lucrative homegrown documentary of all time – which I find somewhat disturbing. A central thesis of the film is that the modern corporation (think post-1900) displays the same pathology as a psychopath. Which is to say that it shows a callous unconcern for the feelings of others, incapacity to maintain enduring relationships, and a reckless disregard for the safety of others, among other sins. I find such a portrayal dangerously misleading.

I have written previously about the ways short-term corporate thinking can shortchange society; in particular, I have argued that the confluence of three trends – corporate autonomy, a digital economy, and naively impatient investors – has created a monster in the form of pressure to produce short-term results. Nowhere is this more evident than in the fallout from ImCone, Tyco, Adelphia, WorldCom, K-Mart, Enron and others. And yes, I think we need to look beyond tighter controls on the accounting and auditing profession, stiffer penalties for offenders and more transparent CEO disclosure of compensation if we are to truly reform the market and the companies that play there. I have a particular interest in examining what the Wall Street scandals mean for the neoclassical theory of the firm and the assumption of profit maximization that underlies it, what the fiduciary requirement for directors to act "in the best interests of the corporation" really mean, and what time scale should be used in measuring the success of a company, and by extension its board and CEO. Still, the suggestion that all (or most) corporations are "externalizing machines", to use one of the film's grim labels, is unfair. There is a world of difference between a smart company that knows it doesn't make sense to close every loop and an externalizing machine. Skeptics might rightly challenge me on this point. Why shouldn't corporations close every loop? Put simply, it isn't necessarily in the public interest for them to do so. *The Corporation* steps blithely past the benefits that accrue to society from industrial activity – benefits that are typically accompanied by some level of pollution (how many zero emission, zero waste companies do you know?). If a firm was compelled to eliminate all pollution or waste; to close every loop, the social costs of doing so could well outweigh the benefits.

The responsibility of business to society has been a persistent theme in the management literature, and for at least three decades there has been a robust debate about the role that business should play in addressing societal problems, particularly environmental problems. No less an authority than Peter Drucker framed the challenge this way:

> This new concept of social responsibility no longer asks what the limitations on business are, or what business should be doing for those under its immediate authority. It demands that business take responsibility for social problems, social issues, social and political goals and that it become the keeper of society's conscience and the solver of society's problems.

The happy news is that more and more corporations have stepped up to the challenge. The World Business Council for Sustainable Development is a notable example. A coalition of 160 international companies united by a shared commitment to sustainable development through economic growth, ecological balance and social progress, it has sparked much-needed thinking about how business can help society shift to a more sustainable trajectory. Yes, the ecological economist in me would like to see more emphasis on "development" than "growth", but I appreciate the effort WBCSD is making. Are some of the members just along for the ride, cloaking themselves in a green veil in the hopes of earning some good PR? Probably. Does it matter? Probably not. The overwhelming majority of WBCSD members are backstopping the good words with tangible actions that are rapidly slaying the myth that one can't be green and competitive. And to those readers who point out that the WBCSD is a rather exclusive club for only the largest of corporations, I would point to the "next generation" of businesses – energetic companies like Antioch, Baxter Healthcare, Fetzer Vineyards, Herman Miller, Organic Valley, Patagonia, and Shorebank Pacific – that are re-writing the rules for their respective sectors. I would add that organizations such as the World Economic Forum have increasingly recognized the importance of sustainability. Finally, business schools worldwide, the gene pool from which the next generation of corporate leaders typically springs, have discovered that more and more students are interested in exploring sustainability – this augurs well for future corporate behavior.

And so, to those who watch *The Corporation* and come away thinking that we need to reform (or blow up) the corporate model, I would say take a deep breath and look at the bigger picture. As with any socially created institution, there are examples of human failing leading to disaster. Equally, there are examples of companies that understand the dynamic interplay of financial, social and environmental aspirations and work hard to achieve results for their shareholders as well as their other stakeholders. These companies endure. They also inspire. Let them guide us in our efforts to improve on the institution of the corporation, but let them also sharpen our will to defend that which is good about corporations. And lest anyone doubt, or forget, there is much to defend. As Jim Collins put it for *Fortune Magazine* recently, "Some of the most amazing inventions in history are not technology or products, they're social inventions. The modern corporation is in that league, not so much because it is a font of technological innovation, but because it is the bridge between market mechanisms and democracy."

Measurement and Management in Business: Toward a New Model of Alignment

Jacques Ancel, the 20th century French scholar, once observed that "it is not the frame that is important, but what is framed". Ancel's interest was political geography, but his observation seems equally valid in the business world – and especially so in the realm of performance measurement. Too many organizations are preoccupied with measures or indicators (the frame) and have inadvertently lost sight of the bigger picture that is their strategy (what is being framed).

It has become something of a mantra if not shibboleth that "what gets measured gets managed". And so it is that managers try to translate their strategic intent into measures or indicators that can be counted, used (one hopes) to improve organizational decisions and performance, and reported to shareholders and other stakeholders.

While the need to measure is intuitively clear, I believe there is a danger in measurement that is often overlooked. The danger springs from a failure to identify measures that are meaningful and rely instead on measures that are easy to assemble, consistent with industry peers, or consistent with past practice. I might add that many organizations compile a dizzying number of measures that creates more confusion than clarity. These dangers are especially evident among advocates of sustainability.

Now, before I step onto the proverbial limb that some readers might want to cut off, let me be clear: I have a keen professional and personal interest in shifting society onto a more sustainable trajectory and I applaud the intellectual and other energy that has given rise to measurement frameworks such as GRI and GPI, and metaphors such as the footprint, barometer and dashboard. My concern is that these efforts, however well-intentioned, have not bridged the gap between what I will call mainstream strategy on the one hand, and sustainability on the other.

If we are to establish measures that "make sense" at a deep strategic level, it seems to me that we should always begin with an organization's strategy. Tony Manning, in his handy treatise, *Making Sense of Strategy* (2002), argued that it is only what is spoken about that will be measured, much less managed. Put another way, it is only what is important to an organization's leaders, what creates and informs the context or "mental space" in which people work that matters. And so the challenge for those with an interest in sustainability is to become more actively involved in strategy creation, or ensure that they have a solid footing on the strategy or point of view that their organization is seeking to deploy. Measurement efforts must take their cue from this strategic line of sight. And of course, because the real world of strategy is less about tiresome annual planning efforts and more about making decisions "on the run", some searching questions should underlie any measurement effort: Will this measure contribute to or advance our strategy? Will this measure be useful and meaningful at different levels in the organization? Are we, the architects of performance measurement (and sustainability), part of an ongoing conversation about what lies ahead for our organization?

There are signs of progress. My concerns aside, GRI and GPI are significant advances over early measures of emissions or outputs. And the importance of considering the entire "web" of supplier and customer relationships is becoming more accepted. But if performance measurement and sustainability are to become part of the strategic firmament, the thinking that underlies them must catch up with current thinking about strategy.

$58 Oil: Save Your Balance Sheet...and the Planet[3]

On Saturday, June 18, 2005 I was struck by two articles that highlight an opportunity to dramatically improve the financial performance of most of the world's businesses, and save the planet in the bargain. The first was a report in *The Globe and Mail* noting that the price of crude oil had surpassed $58 a barrel . The second was a comment in Patagonia's spring catalogue about innovation and sustainability. To the casual reader these may appear to be unrelated items, but they're not. At $58 a barrel, the cost of manufacturing, transporting and servicing virtually any product becomes perilously uneconomic for any business still wedded to fossil fuels. Balance sheets that were already bleeding will now start to hemorrhage. And of course, as many experts have long been telling us, reliance on an energy source that is shredding our planet's life support systems through climate change is the antithesis of prudent risk management. This brings me to Patagonia. Long a pioneer in the outdoor clothing and equipment field, the company also has a distinguished history of genuinely educating customers and other stakeholders on sustainability. Nowhere is this more evident than in the company's newest catalogue. An essay on innovation points out that the challenge for business is no longer simply about finding new ways to solve old problems; it's also about asking whether the innovation is healthy for the environment.

For too long it has been too easy for business not to truly innovate on energy. The price of oil was low, or within an acceptable risk profile and the costs of decarbonization were seen as being unacceptably high. In the face of those hard financial numbers, any additional pleas to altruism or social responsibility fell on deaf ears. Those days are gone. And perhaps that's the silver lining to $58 barrel oil. Perhaps now we can see innovation harnessed to alternative energy. Herewith

[3] First written and posted online (www.abbottstrategies.com) in 2005. Revised and expanded for this publication.

then, a five-point call to action:

- Businesses should quickly develop and incorporate alternative energy rules into all capital expenditures – a condition for any new expenditure is that the energy source be non-carbon; ?
- Energy efficiency must be dramatically promoted in every sector of society – it should become a badge of honor for a business to tout the money it has saved through these efforts;?
- governments across the northern hemisphere should set a target of 50% of all energy being non-carbon; ?
- all vehicle fleets should be transitioned to hybrid and alternative fuel status; and ?
- the big three auto makers in North America need to step up their level of activity on the creation of hybrid and other technologies – these are the energy sources that will fuel the future, but only if the boys in Detroit start to think of them as something other than novelties or curiosities.

Jared Diamond's best-selling new book, *Collapse*, which chronicles the failure of previous civilizations to negotiate a relationship with the Earth that is sustainable, provides a useful point of context as we think about energy and our world. Too many of us live at a remove from nature, a remove that blunts our understanding of nature and our dependence on nature. Too many of us go through our days in a quest for ease, comfort and convenience. And of course, too many of us, especially in North America, are consumers – whose sense of self is defined through the acquisition of stuff – cars, sport utility vehicles, boats, sea-doos and ski-doos[ii]– that perpetuate a dependence on fossil fuels. This dependence is largely responsible for the removal of half the world's original forest cover, the collapse of most of the world's marine fisheries, and the conversion of natural habitats to human-made habitats, notably cities. Recent evidence from the Millennium Ecosystem Assessment research indicates that 60% of the ecosystem services that support life on Earth are being degraded or used unsustainably – 60% ! And there is something more. Walter Youngquist, a geologist who worked for many of the world's major oil companies, tells it well in his book, *GeoDestinies: The Inevitable Control of Earth Resources Over Nations and Individuals.*

> There is no parallel in history for such a rapid development of and use of a resource as in the case of oil…It will be but a brief bright blip on the screen of human history

So, in a very short period of time we have constructed an entire civilization dependent on a finite resource – and a resource whose extraction, development, use and disposal damages essential ecosystem services critical to our long-term survival. As Ronald Wright puts it in *A Short History of Progress:*

> Ecological markers suggest that in the early 1960s, humans were using about 70 per cent of nature's yearly output; by the early 1980s, we'd reached 100 per cent; and in 1999, we were at 125 per cent. Such numbers may be imprecise, but their trend is clear – they mark the road to bankruptcy.

All of this has special relevance in Canada, where our energy industry is centered on the development of heavy oil deposits in Northern Alberta. The development of this particular form of energy, to feed our carbon appetite, comes at a heavy cost. As Andrew Nikiforuk in his inimitable fashion has called it:

> In the past decade, the moral carelessness of the Alberta and federal governments has grown exponentially. As a consequence, even US mayors and British energy consumers are now talking about Canada's "dirty oil", because bitumen, no matter how you spin it, is a corrosive, smog-making, water-fouling, bottom-of-the-barrel product. Make no mistake about it: Canada now faces an intractable political emergency. It can either slow down tar sands development to serve a planned transition to renewable energy sources, or it can rape the world's last great oil field and put the nation on a road to hell.

If the ecological signals didn't convince us previously, maybe the combination of increasingly dire environmental news and oil at $58 a barrel will. Our backs are against the wall and it's time to act – decisively, confidently, without fear. Can we learn from our mistakes – both historical and recent? Can we begin to chart a course that is deliberately different from the civilizations of the past? John Ralston Saul's new book, *The Collapse of Globalism*, argues that we live in a storm between two weather fronts in which nationalism is reasserting domestic interests in both positive and negative ways. This is sustainability on a vast canvas; the argument writ large. And make no mistake; oil figures prominently in our global dilemma. We now stand at a crossroads on our evolutionary path. In one direction lies almost inevitable collapse. In another, lies an exciting future of cleaner air, healthier people, and new types of economic opportunity. I know which path I'll be choosing.

Oil Profits, Global Warming and the Nature of Business

On Tuesday, January 31, 2006 the *Calgary Herald* ran two stories that demonstrated yet again just how ephemeral human civilization might be.

In the first story, we were told that Exxon Mobil, the world's largest publicly traded oil company, posted profits exceeding $10 billion in the last quarter of 2005 – a record for any U.S. company, and a key driver of the largest annual reported net income in U.S. history[iv]. Further, we were told that Exxon's results lifted the combined 2005 profits for the US's three largest oil companies to more than $63 billion. Let me be clear here; I'm talking about profits, the residual when all expenses have been paid.

In the second story, the head of the British Antarctic Survey, Chris Rapley, warned that the huge west Antarctic ice sheet may be disintegrating – a bellwether of climate change and an event that could raise sea levels by five meters.

If we connect these two stories a disturbing and disturbingly familiar pattern emerges. Exxon and its oil industry peers are making money from an energy source (refined hydrocarbons) that is directly responsible for an unsustainable build-up of greenhouse gases in the atmosphere leading to climate change.

At the G8 Summit last June, the leaders of the world's industrialized nations agreed that climate change is happening, that human activity is contributing to it, and that greenhouse gas emissions must decline, moving society toward a low-carbon economy.

And so we return to the unprecedented profits being made by the oil companies. Make no mistake; I have nothing against profits – they are a deserving reward for a successful entrepreneur. But I believe they are also more than that. As Charles Handy put it in a provocative 2002 article for *Harvard Business Review*, "the purpose of a business is not to make a profit, full stop. It is to make a profit so that the business can do something more or better". This something more becomes the real purpose of the business.

Most businesses are managed through the narrow lens of financial performance, a lens that may not adequately identify risks and opportunities. With oil supplies peaking and powerful new economies in China and India accelerating, resource depletion and the corresponding price point escalation will become commonplace. While previously a necessary part of any robust environmental or climate change strategy, a strategic energy management and raw materials plan with an emphasis on decarbonizing supply and value chains now looms as a fundamental business imperative that transcends environmental stewardship.

Easy access to abundant sources of hydrocarbon fuels has created substantial inertia within the industrialized world. Every second, the world consumes 37,000 gallons of oil, 480 tons of coal, and 3 million cubic feet of natural gas. Oil, coal, and natural gas now supply 85% of world energy needs. But what happens in a world market in which hydrocarbons are less abundant and the effects of climate change are felt in more acute ways? The choices that companies like Exxon make in the face of this question will go a long way toward defining the kind of world we live in. Look at it this way, our current addiction to hydrocarbons is unsustainable on two counts: (1) supplies are dwindling; and (2) continued use of these energy sources is damaging the environment beyond the point of repair.

So, how to move forward? To every oil company out there, I say "what percentage of your profits are you reinvesting in an innovation agenda that dramatically accelerates the viability of alternatives to hydrocarbon fuels?" Seventy years ago Joseph Schumpeter defined profit as "the premium put upon successful innovation in capitalist society and [it] is temporary by nature: it will vanish in the subsequent process of competition and adaptation". In an era characterized by dwindling reserves of traditional fuels, increasing evidence of climate change, and hypercompetition, it seems clear that a portion of any oil company's profits needs to be reinvested in activities that deliberately push the envelope of the firm's business model – or indeed the conventional wisdom of the industry itself.

Henry Hubble, Exxon's VP of Investor Relations, attributes his firm's success to its ability to create "world-class projects". While the context needs to change, and change quickly, the spirit of those words has never been truer. Time to step up to the plate, Mr. Hubble, and use some of those profits to do "something more", to create world-class projects that facilitate a global shift to alternative energy

Disconnect in Reporting on Oil, Hybrids

A recent edition of *Report on Business* in the *Globe and Mail* contained two articles that underscore how far we have yet to travel if we are to wean ourselves off oil – and in doing so, forge an exciting new future of cleaner air, healthier people, and new types of economic opportunity.

In "India tells West: Take our oil, please", we were told that Indian Oil Minister, Mani Shankar Aiyar, is criss-crossing the globe (no doubt burning many barrels of oil) in an effort to encourage oil and gas investment in his country. Soaring economic growth in India is creating a huge appetite for energy. Nothing wrong with that, but why is the default position oil? Okay, I know that demand for energy in India far outstrips the supply of clean, green energy alternatives. And of course, with an estimated ¼ trillion barrels of oil and gas just offshore, India sees a comparatively easy solution. Economy growing like a rocket, and with it the need for energy? No problem, we've got boatloads of oil just offshore. The problem is that exploiting the oil and gas perpetuates a global malaise – reliance on an energy source that is shredding our planet's life support systems through climate change, and accelerating the deaths of thousands of people each year who choke on the emissions of cars and trucks, particularly in the world's cities. Why not position oil and gas as a transition fuel for India and earmark a portion of the profits from its use for investment in cleaner alternatives? I have nothing against Minister Aiyar stumping for investment, but I'd like to see him and his colleagues frame the energy problem more strategically.

In many respects, the same thinking that has spurred oil and gas investment at the expense of other energy options cropped up in the other ROB story, "Hybrids won't dominate market, study predicts". Here, the good people at J.D. Power & Associates told us that despite increasing popularity, hybrid vehicles will peak at roughly 3% of the U.S. automobile market by 2010. Regrettably, the article didn't tell us anything about the method used to generate that estimate, but no matter, if it's even close to being accurate, we've got a problem, a big one. Why is it that lifestyle aspirations and choices in the U.S. (and I would argue Canada is similar) run against nature? The answer must be more than a failure to "get the price signals right". On a global scale, we have failed as a society to make the connections between social and economic well-being and nature both obvious and important to more than a green constituency. And so it is that India is shopping around for partners to exploit oil and gas while hybrid vehicles that might help shift society onto a cleaner, healthier trajectory languish.

I would have hoped that by now it was obvious that the complex patterns of interaction that characterize biological and human systems cry out for new ideas. Evidently, there is still much to be done. Accordingly, as a country, and as a participant on the global stage, Canada must begin to dramatically increase the "nature literacy" of people here at home and around the world. To paraphrase our own Rick Mercer in his delightful series of commercials promoting Canada's 1-tonne challenge to reduce greenhouse gases, "if we could see greenhouse gases, we'd be screaming for change". We need to make people aware of the true costs of energy and point out that non-carbon alternatives are available that won't cramp anyone's style. More to the point, we need to start thinking about hybrid and other technologies as something more than novelties or curiosities – they're going to fuel the future, but only if we start to think of them in that light.

NOTES TO SECTION 3

[i] Following the rise to $58 a barrel, the rate of increase slowed somewhat. By January 2007, the price of a barrel of oil was below $60, but unprecedented increases were not far off. By early 2008, the price of a barrel had exceeded $100 for the first time, and by mid-July 2008, it had risen to an al-time record of $147 a barrel – early 3 times the price that first galvanized me to write the piece included in this collection. By the end of August 2008, the price had backed off to $115 a barrel. At this price level, the central argument of my paper – that the cost of extracting resources, manufacturing products, transporting those products to markets, and so is a fool's game. It is time to accelerate investment in carbon-free sources of energy.As the noted investor and philanthropist, George Soros, has put it: "In contrast to oil and other fossil fuels whose costs of production are bound to rise, the alternative fuels will become cheaper as we discover cheaper and more efficient technologies to exploit them."

[ii] Jonathan Porritt reminds us of a compelling point in this regard in his book, Capitalism as if the World Matters: "There are clearly enormous differences in different people's material aspirations.

Although there is still serious poverty in almost all OECD countries, what are defined as 'basic human needs' are now largely met in those countries. But as far back as 1930, John Maynard Keynes pointed out that our *absolute* wants (those which we feel regardless of our relative position in society) are limited and finite; it is our *relative* wants (those which we feel in comparison to what others have in society) that are apparently insatiable – and it is these relative wants that keep the wheels of our growth machine spinning merrily away".

[iii] The dependence on fossil fuels, and consumption patterns in North America, and for the most part, other northern hemisphere countries, are also responsible for meager progress against the United Nations Millennium Development Goals. As the *United Nations Human Development Report*, 2005 put it: "In the midst of an increasingly prosperous global economy, 10.7 million children every year do not live to see their fifth birthday, and more than 1 billion people survive in abject poverty on less than $1 a day. One fifth of humanity live in countries where many people think nothing of spending $2 a day on a cappuccino. Another fifth of humanity survive on less than a dollar a day, and live in countries where children die for want of a simple anti-mosquito net.

[iv] The money keeps rolling in for Exxon. Profits in 2007 and 2008 continued to grow to unprecedented levels.

Renewal

We are now faced with the fact my friends that tomorrow is today. We are confronted with the fierce urgency of now. In this unfolding conundrum of life and history, there is such a thing as being too late.

—Martin Luther King

. . . In our house, I was always the first out of bed. Getting the coffee on, reading the newspaper. A quiet ritual while the rest of the house slept. He would join me and together we'd carry our mugs into the garden. Nothing fancy, just a couple of chairs surrounded by peonies. We went outside so our voices wouldn't disturb the others. But also, to drink in the smell of morning. Sweet, still air, perfumed by flowers, coffee, soil and pipe tobacco. Another ritual. We both loved to talk, but these mornings were, ultimately, about stillness, quiet observation. Grass stretching, dew turning to steam. Arrows of sun bringing light to the edge of our forest. A world of activity unfolding before our eyes. All because of our rituals. Simple things, that are not simple at all. They contain the world.

Seeing the World with New Eyes: Hortus Cultura in a Discordant Age[1]

The poet and gardener, Patrick Lane, begins his award-winning memoir, *There is a Season*, with a quote that serves as a potent distillation of much that I want to share with you this morning. He says "If what we know is what resembles us, what we know is a garden." I draw both strength and, dare I say it, a certain melancholy from these words. The strength comes from the reminder that we are all, ultimately, part of nature. The melancholy soon follows because too few of us know this, or accept this. And so to the title of my remarks: *"Seeing the World with New Eyes: Hortus Cultura in a Discordant Age"*.

Over half the world's population now lives in cities – human-made habitats, and with technological innovations continually flowering from fertile minds, some have asked if the human species even "needs" nature. They can be forgiven for asking the apocryphal question. We do, after all, live in an era of unprecedented innovation. And yet, despite our intellectual prowess, the gift that sets us apart from other species, we do not understand the world around us. Too many of us live at a remove from nature, a remove that blunts our understanding of nature and our dependence on nature. Too many of us go through our days in a quest for ease, comfort and convenience. And of course, too many of us, especially in North America, are consumers – whose sense of self is defined through the acquisition of stuff – more and bigger cars, bigger houses, better clothes. It is like the close of the nineteenth century all over again, a time when wealthy Londoners felt they had to demonstrate their wealth through conspicuous consumption.

This culture of more, not less, creates discord. It also creates the need to see our world with new eyes – a poet's eyes, a gardener's eyes. The increasing segregation of people, especially in our cities – by age, family status, education and income exacerbates the discord. Worse, our collective lack of understanding has brought us to either the edge of an abyss, or to a fork in our evolutionary path – we have

[3] Keynote Speech delivered at Kwantlen University College, Vancouver, CANADA, June 14, 2005.

begun to shred the tapestry of natural capital on which we depend. To arrest these changes and forge a new relationship with nature, to choose a path that embodies a more sustainable relationship with the Earth, we must create a spark that excites and engages more than a green constituency; we must create novel partnerships among both experts and non-experts; champion trans-disciplinary work; and raise the nature "literacy" of the people with whom we interact. We must also, crucially, accept and rejoice that we are nature.

Soon, you will disperse to focus on such topical horticultural issues as water conservation, pest management, and the challenge of enhancing British Columbia's garden image. Before you do that however, before you dive into the necessary detail, I want to provoke you, and I want to encourage you. I'm going to talk about four things this morning: (i) the meaning of sustainability; (ii) disconnects that limit our progress in moving toward sustainability; (iii) questions for the horticulture profession arising from these first two pieces of discussion; and (iv) some thoughts on the way forward. In doing this, I want to provoke you to think about your profession differently, to ask different kinds of questions of each other. And I want to encourage you to think about the art of the possible. Great things happen when people imagine what's possible. What is the story you are creating today? What are the values that inform it? How are you going to communicate your results today, and to whom? I think all of us here this morning value the physical environment that underpins our lives in British Columbia. We value the mountains, the clean air, the weather, the open space, and the quality of life. We also value our physical health and wellbeing. I want you to tap into these fundamental values and use them as a lens through which to view your work. I want you to follow the game, not the ball; to keep your brainstorming today rooted in a healthy appreciation for the course you and your profession are traveling through time. Because, ultimately, there is only one question for you today: Where are we going?

Context: What is Sustainability?

In the closing years of the 20th century, human concern over the consequences of production and consumption decisions – growth if you prefer previously a niche discussion, became a conspicuous feature on the cultural landscape and the subject of much academic and popular discussion. As we begin the 21st century, the relationships between environmental protection, economic development, and social welfare are being explored and debated with great fervor around the world. These relationships, commonly called sustainability, were first cited under that moniker in the *World Conservation Strategy* in 1980, introduced to a wider audience in the report of the World Commission on Environment and Development (WCED) in 1987, and further elaborated at the United Nations Conferences on Environment and Development (UNCED) in Rio de Janeiro in 1992, and Johannesburg in 2002 – the so-called Earth Summits.

In the same year as the Rio Earth Summit, the Union of Concerned Scientists sent the *World Scientists' Warning to Humanity* for endorsement to all scientists worldwide who had been awarded the Nobel Prize, and to national academy-level scientists in Africa, Canada, China, Europe, India, Japan, Latin America, Russia, the United Kingdom, and the United States. The Warning, signed by over 1700 scientists, including a majority of Nobel Laureates, was a passionate argument for sustainability. It said, in part:

> We the undersigned, senior members of the world's scientific community, hereby warn all humanity of what lies ahead. A great change in our stewardship of the earth and the life on it is required, if vast human misery is to be avoided and our global home on this planet is not to be irretrievably mutilated.

Five actions were identified to shift society's trajectory onto a more favorable plane:

- Bring environmentally damaging activities under control to restore and protect the integrity of the earth's systems
- Manage resources crucial to human welfare more effectively
- Stabilize population
- Reduce and eventually eliminate poverty

- Ensure sexual equality, and guarantee women control over their own reproductive decisions

These actions struck at three related and fundamental themes: (1) the criticality of the Earth's natural systems as the basis for life; (2) the need to stabilize population to avoid "overshooting" the ability of natural systems to support human life; and (3) the relationship between resources and poverty. To a large degree society continues to struggle in making progress on these actions. The late, lamented Dana Meadows amplified the UCS message in a monograph published shortly before her death. She said:

The world economy is doubling roughly every twenty years. The world population is doubling every forty to fifty years. The planet that supplies the materials and energy necessary for the functioning of the population and economy is not growing at all. That means whatever planetary resource was one-fourth-used a generation ago is half-used today. Whatever waste sink was half-full a generation ago is full today. Whatever was full a generation ago is overfull today.

In some respects, Meadows' argument is reminiscent of the character in Ernest Hemingway's novel, *The Sun Also Rises* (1926), who is asked how he went bankrupt. Two ways, he says: gradually and then suddenly. If, despite education, technology, and other features of contemporary society, humankind's production and consumption habits threaten or outstrip life-sustaining habitat, the trajectory is not sustainable. To survive, much less prosper, the trajectory must be changed. It is to this end that considerable effort has been spent in recent years elucidating the idea of sustainability.

There is no universally accepted definition of sustainability. In fact, many are tiring of the term arguing that it can be spun to reflect any number of different agendas. While it is tempting to acquiesce in the face of such arguments, a review of sustainability initiatives throughout the world suggests that it is generally understood to be a roadmap for human development that recognizes the importance and interdependence of environmental, social and economic well-being (see table 2). A partial typology of the arguments and positions includes proponents of "weak" sustainability, who believe that as long as the total stock of natural and human-made capital does not decrease between generations the conditions for sustainability have been met. It would also include advocates of "strong" sustainability, who believe human-made capital cannot be wholly substituted for natural capital. David Pearce, Professor of Economics at University College, London and Director of the London Environmental Economics Center, defined sustainability as a "wealth inheritance – a stock of knowledge and understanding, a stock of technology, a stock of man-made capital and a stock of environmental assets – no less than that inherited by the current generation." The Swedish oncologist and environmental scientist, Karl-Henrik Robert, has spoken passionately about what he calls the resource "funnel" as a metaphor for the sustainability challenge. As he sees it, shrinking resource supplies coupled to rising consumption creates a funnel in which society exceeds its carrying capacity. He has proposed a series of system conditions, popularly known as The Natural Step, to lead society out of the funnel. In table 2, the key theme or intellectual contribution from a global scan of sustainability principles or codes of practice is summarized.

At least two things stand out in considering these principles and ideas; the first is the diversity of thought. The second is the hierarchy of principles governing sustainability. At least six "core" principles cut across all three dimensions of sustainability and are distinctively holistic:

- Ecological limits
- Interdependence
- Precautionary principle
- Adaptive management
- Stakeholder view
- Equity

Ecological limits speaks to the idea that since the Earth is not growing in size human society must be careful about its use of resources and generation of wastes, lest the global system be overwhelmed. In a business context, this principle compels firms to protect natural capital. In a pulp and paper context, for example, conformance with AOX targets and stewardship of other liquid and atmospheric discharges, as well as energy and water consumption are some of the ways in which individual mill or company performance can erode or protect natural capital.

Interdependence postulates that financial and social wealth or prosperity is dependent on natural capital. Erosions in the productive or aesthetic capacity of natural capital will therefore erode financial and social capital. If fiber supply for pulp and paper mills is systematically reduced

Table 2: Sustainability in Microcosm: Overarching Themes in Sustainability Principles and Codes of Practice

Sustainability Principle or Code of Practice	Key Overarching Theme or New Contribution to Discourse
• The Tokyo Declaration (1987)	• Quality of growth
• The CERES Principles (1989)	• Top management accountability
• Principles of Sustainable Development from Herman Daly (1990)	• Sustainability applied to renewable and nonrenewable resources and pollutants (ecological limits)
• ICC Business Charter for Sustainable Development (1991)	• Precautionary principle
• The Hannover Principles (1991)	• Interdependence
• IUCN, UNEP, WWF Principles (1991, revised 1996)	• Ecological limits
• The Rio Declaration (1992)	• Global covenant on sustainability
• United Church of Canada Statement of Ethical Principles for Environment and Development (1992)	• Global perspective; non-violent conflict resolution; participatory decision-making
• Principles of Sustainability from Stephen Schmidheiny (1992)	• Precautionary principle; "no regrets" policies
• BCNI Business Principles for a Sustainable and Competitive Future (1992)	• Sustainability as key operating principle for companies (goals, objectives, measures)
• Principles of Sustainability from Lester Brown (1992)	• State of the world critique (species loss, soil, forest loss, fish harvests, population)
• NRTEE Principles of Sustainability (1994)	• Preservation of capacity of biosphere; shared responsibility
• City of Portland Sustainable City Principles (1994)	• Cumulative and long-term impacts; long-term environmental and operating costs
• IDRC Principles of Sustainability (1994)	• Ecological limits; dynamic nature of ecosystem functioning; protection of biodiversity
• North American Regional Consultation on Sustainable Livelihoods (1995)	• Reduce travel to workplace; generate social returns; value non-monetized work
• Le Projet de Societe (1995)	• Social, interregional and intergenerational equity
• President's Council on Sustainable Development Principles (1995)	• Ecological limits an issue of national and global security; technology as lever; trade and economic development as unavoidable subjects
• Bellagio Principles for Sustainable Development (1996)	• Thematic presentation; whole system thinking; state, direction and rate of change in state of capital stocks
• Earth Charter Benchmark Principles of Sustainable Development (1996)	• International relations perspective; polluter pays; transfer of capability and capacity
• The Sustainable Society Project (1996)	• Preserve capacity for system to change
• State of Minnesota Sustainable Development Initiative (1999)	• Natural capital as basis for financial and social prosperity as well as liberty
• The Resort Municipality of Whistler Environmental Strategy (1999)	• Aesthetic values
• State of Oregon Executive Order on Sustainability (2000)	• Voluntary systems; linkage between resource use and environmental health
• Earth Charter of Maurice Strong (2000)	• Consolidation of ideas expressed in 1972 and 1992 UN "Earth Summits"
• World Religions Pledge for Action on Conservation (2000)	• Sacred gifts for a living planet

This table is not intended to be an exhaustive inventory of sustainability principles or codes of practice, but rather, a guide to the range of thinking on the subject.

because of excess harvests, the capacity of the mill to create financial or social wealth is compromised.

The precautionary principle states that the environment should not be left to show harm before action is taken to protect it. The history of human–environment relations shows that variability and unpredictability in ecosystem functioning have repeatedly confounded management efforts. Ecosystems should therefore be viewed as dynamic systems, and an effort should be made to continually improve human understanding of ecosystem functioning, and decisions with irreversible consequences should be avoided.

Adaptive management is an approach to natural capital decisions in which each decision is approached in an experimental manner – the existing state, direction and rate of change in state of the capital stock is continually monitored, and feedback allows adjustments in decisions to be made.

Stakeholder view acknowledges that anyone who can affect, or be affected by, the products and services of an entity should be engaged in decisions about how that entity will operate. In a business context, this principle expands considerably on the traditional shareholder view to include employees, customers, strategic partners, and others along the supply and value chains .

Equity is about fairness; the financial and social wealth that is created through the use of natural capital, and indeed the natural capital stock itself, should be shared in a manner that is fair from the perspective of each stakeholder group.

Several other "supporting" principles are narrower in scope, attaching to the economic, social or environmental domain (see table 3).

Regardless of how much, or little, enthusiasm you can muster for any of these principles, it is important to note that some prominent environmental intellectuals are wary of the way in which "sustainability" has been framed, especially by the business community. In his thoughtful essay on the prospects for sustainability of British Columbia forests, *Reinventing British Columbia: Towards a New Political Economy in the Forest*, Michael M'Gonigle opined that if there is to be sustainability, society must begin by rejecting the oxymoron of sustainable development:

Table 3: Hierarchy of Sustainability Principles

CORE SUSTAINABILITY PRINCIPLES		
	Ecological limits Interdependence Precautionary principle Adaptive management Stakeholder view Equity	
SUPPORTING PRINCIPLES		
ECONOMIC	**SOCIAL**	**ENVIRONMENTAL**
▪ Quality of economic life ▪ Full-cost assessment ▪ Valuation of non-monetized work	▪ Quality of society ▪ Participatory decision-making ▪ Shared responsibility	▪ Quality of the environment ▪ Cumulative effects ▪ Synergistic effects ▪ Aesthetic values

> Development in the traditional mode is simply not compatible with the constraints of environmentalism. In its place, we must turn this concept [sustainable development] around, and begin to "develop sustainably". In this formulation, "they get the verb and we get the object".

While his use of the "us versus them" dialectic betrays an allegiance to the environmental community, many share M'Gonigle's passion and position. In his trenchant 1998 book, Upside Down: A Primer for the Looking Glass World, the Uruguayan writer, Eduardo Galeano, was profoundly skeptical of corporate efforts to become sustainable. "The earths most successful companies have offices in hell and heaven too". Given corporate behavior through history, and the belief by many that society doesn't have much time to realign its production and consumption patterns to accord with ecological limits, the skepticism is perhaps understandable. Against this backdrop, John Ehrenfeld, Director of the Program on Technology, Business and the Environment at MIT, and Executive Director of the International Society for Industrial Ecology, has drawn a metaphorical line in the sand with his observation that :

> I define sustainability as the possibility that humans and other life forms will flourish on the earth forever. Flourishing means not only survival, but also the realization of whatever we as

> humans declare makes life good and meaningful, including notions like justice, freedom, and dignity. And as a possibility, sustainability is a guide to actions that will or can achieve its central vision of flourishing for time immemorial…It is a future vision from which we can construct our present way of being.

Disconnects Inhibiting Sustainability

At the close of his eloquent disquisition on biodiversity, *The Diversity of Life*, E.O. Wilson suggests that time is slipping away from us, and with it, the ability to arrest the loss of biodiversity and understand the world around us. While human ingenuity has flowered magnificently, the paradox of our evolution is that our progress has begun to imperil the "natural capital" on which we depend. Where is the human-made analogue for photosynthesis that can maintain the balance of carbon dioxide and oxygen in the atmosphere, or a filtration device that mimics the roots of trees and other plants and filters heavy metals and other toxic contaminants from our water?

Many of you will be familiar with Jared Diamond's bestselling book, *Collapse*, which chronicles the failure of previous civilizations to negotiate a relationship with the Earth that is sustainable. Ronald Wright made a similar, and to my mind at least, even more persuasive argument in his Massey Lectures from 2004, *A Short History of Progress*. And John Ralston Saul is climbing the bestseller lists with his new book, *The Collapse of Globalism*, in which he argues that we live in a storm between two weather fronts in which nationalism is reasserting domestic interests in both positive and negative ways. This is sustainability on a vast canvas; the argument writ large. Can we learn from our mistakes – both historical and recent? Can we begin to chart a course that is deliberately different from the civilizations of the past, or indeed different from our predecessors at the beginning of the 20th century – arguably the last time unregulated markets and dispossessed citizens collided? Time will tell. In my darker and more pessimistic moments, I am reminded of Eugene O'Neil's comment that there is no present or future, only the past, happening over and over again. These moments tend to be spurred by what I perceive as disconnects in our media and popular culture. Let me give you two quick examples.

In an editorial published last Fall, the *Calgary Herald* that took issue with a research project that sought to measure the ecological footprint (the cumulative resources necessary to support each citizen) of 20 Canadian cities. At nearly 10 hectares per person, Calgary exceeded the Canadian average of 7.25. The editorial defended the status quo, arguing that while Calgary consumes a lot of resources, it "bakes a bigger pie" for more people to eat. Further and most crucially, the editorial asserted that to reduce the city's footprint it is necessary to "kill growth" – an assertion that misses two important points about the metaphor of the footprint, and the larger objective of sustainability. First, it is less about shaming us for our resource consumption and more about sparking innovation in how we think about, measure and improve our economic, social and environmental performance. Second, reductions in a city's footprint do not automatically mean a drop in welfare. In fact, there is a growing body of evidence that suggests the opposite may be true. A 2001 study by the Pembina Institute for Appropriate Development, one of Canada's premier environmental NGOs, found that despite steady GDP growth in Alberta since 1982, average real disposable income and real weekly wages, adjusted for inflation, have remained virtually unchanged. Meantime, per capita taxes have increased nearly 500% since 1961, and household debt exceeds disposable income. Maybe those pies aren't so big after all? Maybe we need a better analytical frame to contain more of the costs and benefits of our current growth path? Further, two different national surveys recently found that the unhappiest Canadians live in cities where income is highest. Proof again that as a measure of overall well-being, economic growth and income alone are poor benchmarks.

We need to resist the seduction of easy measures of wealth such as GDP or income because they lead us into what Ronald Wright artfully calls "progress traps":

> "A small village on good land beside a river is a good idea; but when the village grows into a city and paves over the

> good land, it becomes a bad idea. While prevention might have been easy, a cure may be impossible – a city isn't easily moved."

When an economy grows beyond a certain threshold the additional benefits of growth are often exceeded by costs that aren't seen or counted until it's too late. As a result, it is instructive to supplement traditional measures of wealth with such things as the costs of crime, family breakdown, resource depletion and pollution. These "genuine progress" measures strive to offer a more complete picture of wellbeing. Footprint studies such as the one sponsored by FCM are useful as a guide to city activities that are big resource consumers or sinks – and that represent opportunities for innovation. That's right; innovation. Discussions of our relationship to nature and how we might reconfigure economic activity to better accord with nature should not be viewed as anti-development; quite the contrary. The economy can, and should, continue to develop, but it must shift to conceptions of wealth that are not defined by conventional metrics but by a throughput of matter-energy that is within the regenerative and assimilative capacities of the ecosystem.

At the close of the 19th century, Thorsten Veblen, in his masterful, *The Theory of the Leisure Class*, described how wealthy Londoners felt they had to demonstrate their wealth through conspicuous consumption. At the beginning of the 21st century we have come a long way toward understanding the consequences of our consumption choices – partly through the use of tools such as the ecological footprint. Calgary should use the FCM study to broaden its vision from a primary focus on the size of the pie to a more holistic view of the ways in which that pie is baked. Now that's a recipe for real success.

The second example of a disconnect is a 2005 study by the Toronto Board of Health and Environment Canada pointing out that over 1600 people die each year in Toronto and Montreal (over 800 in each city) because of poor air quality. It is tempting to call this an environmental story, but that is too limiting. It is a social and economic story as well – quite apart from the number of deaths, think about those who don't die, but are hospitalized at considerable personal and societal cost to treat respiratory problems. To date, few have begun to connect the dots I'm outlining here, but I'm hopeful that we might still begin to frame the problem properly – and in doing so, recognize that sustainability permeates every aspect of our world, and that understanding it requires new, bold, radical thinking.

Link to Think Tank

So what might all of this mean for the horticulture profession? At one level of analysis, you need to understand how to manage land, water and other resources in ways that are sustainable. You also need to understand community and stakeholder expectations with respect to sustainability – is there a shared vision around which people can rally? And those stakeholders need to learn about horticultural issues in ways that encourage their active, engaged participation. At another, and far more important level of analysis, you need to think about the analytical framework that informs (or should inform) everything you do, and might do differently in the future. Put another way, can you truly see in three dimensions? Or more accurately, can you see across three dimensions? What is your strategy to be a genuine steward of natural capital, and how will this affect both your short-term financial requirements and the perspectives of your stakeholders? How will you protect biodiversity? How will you leave the next generation of horticulturalists with an asset base, in the broadest and richest sense, at least as healthy, diverse and productive as that which you enjoy today? And returning to a question I posed at the beginning of my remarks, what is the nature of the story you want to create today and how will you communicate it?

The Way Forward

Robert Altman's wonderfully cynical film about the movie business, *The Player*, contains an essential truth about stories that may be instructive in this regard. In the film, the central character is asked why a particular screenplay wasn't filmed. He says it lacked certain qualities necessary to make a commercially successful movie. There is a pause.

He expands on his answer. He says up, as opposed to down; happy as opposed to sad; hopeful as opposed to desperate; and a happy ending...especially a happy ending. His point is that while all people like stories; most people like stories that offer hope – and a happy ending. Stories in which good triumphs over evil. Stories propelled by an engaging and entertaining narrative – the route to the happy ending matters.

Now consider the way in which the sustainability "story" has been told. Is it any wonder the majority of people have tuned out? What about the sustainable horticulture story? We need to forge a story about sustainability that hasn't been told yet (or told well). We need to shape a compelling vision of the future, and sell that vision with the kind of passion, money and marketing savvy that Hollywood sells movies. We need to convince people through the art of storytelling that this vision is worth fighting for. And it's okay if the story seems strange – this is what will first take hold of us (and others) and make us believe it.

Nothing happens without first a dream. My dream is a world in which human society lives in a more sustainable relationship with the Earth, and with each other. To get there, we need to write a new story – a story about the future and what can be done now to secure it. We also need to sell this story in ways that heretofore have been overlooked by the sustainability community. We have a great cause; what we lack is a story to grow the constituency of supporters for that cause.

The opening words of a 16th century Polish church-song, Already it is Dusk, describe a fervent prayer for deliverance from evil-doers and the powers of darkness. However much we might like to disagree, we are the evil-doers, those who have brought the Earth to its knees in our headlong rush along the evolutionary corridor to higher levels of consumption. As we look to the future, let us lead with both our head and our heart and make the smart choices that define a new relationship with nature. Let us follow Henry David Thoreau's example and learn the language of the fields that we may better express ourselves.

Our head should compel us to be smart, to make prudent decisions that are not irreversible and to try and improve our understanding of nature. This will require new forms of partnership between both expert and non-expert stakeholders. It will also require the intellectual leadership to champion trans-disciplinary work, something that is too often marginalized if not punished in academia.

Our heart should compel us to honor the birthplace of our spirit and the children who will follow us. We may never solve the mystery that is the green pre-human Earth, but we must allow others to try.

To begin this journey, we should define a vision of our organization, project, or community as sustainable and ask what we would do that is different from what we do now. This vision should be a manifesto for change that catalyzes critical and creative thinking. Among the questions to consider are:

- Why does my horticulture firm exist? What am I producing or creating that is truly of value to the community of which I am a part?
- Am I changing or even challenging the mainstream horticulture profession and its dogma, or am I content to do the occasional boutique project?
- What does sustainability mean to my colleagues and me?
- How do (or should) we engage our customers and partners in a meaningful discussion of sustainable horticulture?
- How should we think about and measure success?

Our willingness to ask searching questions about what we do and why we do it; our willingness to engage our students in a different kind of learning; and our willingness to accept that there are many ways of knowing should shape our ability to meet the design challenges of an era that is characterized by economic, social and environmental change. Put another way, it will determine if we can, as Proust would have us, "see with new eyes" and frame our challenges to accord with the principles of sustainability.

Confronting Ridiculous "Truths"

The March 4th, 2006 edition of *The Globe and Mail* contained at least 3 articles that made me want to channel Howard Beale, the hero of Sidney Lumet's visionary film, Network, who screamed "I'm mad as hell and I'm not going to take it anymore!" Let me explain.

In "Your own one-tonne challenge", Tim Flannery, one of Australia's leading environmental thinkers and writers, argued that in a matter of decades one of every five living things will become extinct unless we wean ourselves off fossil fuels. Yes, it's another story about climate change, but the article, an excerpt from Flannery's new book, *The Weather Makers*, does everything except make your eyes glaze; it's a riveting piece. All the more so because it is clear that we are at a hinge point in history: "we are the generation fated to live in the most interesting of times, for we are now the weather makers, and the future of biodiversity and civilization hangs on our actions...if humans pursue a business-as-usual course for the first half of this century...the collapse of civilization due to climate change becomes inevitable." I can only hope that Flannery's prose makes a sufficiently large number of people ditch their second (or third) car and start boning up on ways and means to reduce their fossil fuel footprint.

In "Cancer, and the battle after", CBC journalist Wendy Mesley talked about her battle with cancer and her investigation into why it is one of Canada's fastest-growing medical crises. The Canadian Cancer Society (CCS) reports that 2,865 Canadians are diagnosed with cancer each week - and 1,337 die. The incidence of cancer in Canada has climbed from 1 in 10 in the 1950s to 1 in 5 in the 1970s to 1 in 2 today. What's going on? Why are we not talking about this more? Why do we seem willing to accept a five-fold increase in the rate of cancer? Well it is probably fair to say that we are more adept at diagnosing cancer today, I can't help but think that we are also living in an increasingly toxic environment that is challenging us, and changing us on a molecular level. And there's some evidence I may be right. A recent editorial in *The Calgary Herald* noted that the CCS is undertaking research into a link between environmental chemical exposure and acute lymphoblastic leukemia, a common childhood cancer. Elizabeth Guilette, a researcher at the University of Florida, has already discovered a disturbing relationship between pesticide exposure and childhood health. In Mexico, children exposed to pesticides had more mental and neuromuscular defects, reduced stamina, and increased respiratory infections. In a country where gardening is a national pastime, we should all think about this the next time we head to the store to pick up supplies to keep our flowers and lawns looking sharp.

In "China keeps bad company", reporter Geoffrey York noted that China's financial support is propping up some of the world's most reprehensible regimes. "With its newfound economic muscle and its amoral zeal to do business with anyone, China is propping up a host of tyrants and dictators who might not otherwise be around." And so it is that China adopts a "business is business" posture and deals with Sudan, Uzbekistan, Iran, North Korea, Myanmar, Angola and Zimbabwe, to name a few.

So there you have it; one newspaper, one day, and 3 articles that got under my skin. They did so because it seems to me that we've become so inured to bad news that we accept it as inevitable or dare I say it, the truth of how things are. Well, I don't accept it. And I certainly don't accept that trend is destiny. I choose to believe that we can do something about climate change. I choose to believe that we can do a better job of cancer prevention rather than treatment after the fact. I choose to believe that we can confront China; call it on behavior that is, frankly, reprehensible and not in the interest of the global commons. Most of all, I choose not to accept that a certain amount of "bad" is inevitable in society. Like John Ralston Saul, I'm amazed, and saddened, by the extent to which our society accepts serious levels of poverty, exclusion and homelessness. There is no reason to accept these things as "truths" of how things are, or must be. There is no need, and certainly no good, in intellectually reconfiguring them as conditions of society.

It's time to challenge what I will charitably call "ridiculous truths" and get on with the work of dreaming big and making those dreams a reality. It's time to remember heroes like the brave women who stood in the rain outside the White House in the early 1960s and brought an end to aboveground nuclear testing and with it, the radioactive fallout that was showing up in mother's milk and baby teeth. The Women's Strike for Peace, and the spirit, the hope that informed it is one of the lights that should guide us out of our current darkness. It's time to remember that we can change the way things are. We can change them to the way things ought to be.

Civic Leadership and the Common Good[2]

I read Michael Robinson's editorial in these pages ("Where best to serve the common good") on March 20, 2006 with considerable interest. Like him, I attended the 7th LaFontaine-Baldwin lecture - a stirring and poetic call to civic engagement by George Elliott Clarke - and like him, I care passionately about what is necessary to "best be a citizen" in pursuit of our national dream. His distillation of Clarke's lecture, and the town hall that followed it, raises many interesting ideas with respect to civic engagement and the role of non-government organizations (NGO) and government agencies and serves as a useful jumping off point to consider where and how we can all contribute to the communities of which we are a part.

Canada today is a country stretching from the Atlantic to the Pacific to the Arctic, but at Confederation in 1867, it ended at the Great Lakes. Canadian visionaries saw the railway as a way to ensure Canada survived American expansion - it would quite literally bind us together as a nation. For its time, the CPR was audacious, a national dream indeed. And a dream that responded to arguably the defining challenge of the day. But that was then; what about now? Today it might well be argued that the role of cities in supporting citizens to lead lives of abundance, lives of access and opportunity, is our defining challenge and a worthy successor to our initial national dream.. Getting there requires much more than merely government or NGO involvement.

Citizens of Canada have a great many rights that give them freedoms we should all hold dear - the freedom to think what we like; to voice those opinions; to worship, or not to worship at all; and so on.

---

[2] This piece was first published in the Calgary Herald in 2006.

However, democratic theory holds that these rights come with responsibilities - to obey laws; to pay taxes; to serve on juries; to exercise the right to vote; etc. The responsibility that can make the most lasting difference, however, is getting involved in the political and policy process. As Craig Rimmerman notes in his book *The New Citizenship: Unconventional Politics, Activism and Service*, "increased citizen participation in community and workplace decision-making is important if people are to recognize their roles and responsibilities as citizens within the larger community...In a true participatory setting, citizens do not merely act as autonomous individuals pursuing their own interests, but instead, through a process of decision, debate, and compromise, they ultimately link their concerns with the needs of the community." *This* is how we can best be a citizen of our country, of our city. This is how we serve the common good. We need to put aside (or at least complement) our individual aspirations and get involved in shaping a truly democratic community. Each of us has a voice and each of us has a responsibility to use that voice to demonstrate that the common good lives in all of us.

I would add that an appreciation for the past, for history, is fundamental in shaping this kind of involvement. Why? As John Ralston Saul noted in the first LaFontaine-Baldwin lecture in 2000, "the past is not the past. It is the context. The past - memory - is one of the most powerful, practical tools available to a civilized democracy... It reminds us of our successes and failures, of their context; it warns us, encourages us."

Consider Stampede – arguably the defining feature of our city's economic and cultural history. Stampede rightly honors the legacy of Guy Weadick, and justly celebrates the pioneer spirit of those who came before us. But is there something more to talk about? Most of the people wearing ten-gallon hats during Stampede are wearing a costume, not an essential part of their daily wardrobe. Farming and ranching might be billion dollar industries here, but energy swamps them. Nearly 70% of the province's annual exports, and a third of all revenue collected by the provincial government, are energy-related.

Stampede grew out of Guy Weadick's desire to do something that hadn't been done before – to stage a rodeo and Wild West event that would draw the best cowboys from across the continent to Calgary. It was an early example of visionary civic leadership in service of something bigger than any one person. The twinning of Stampede with the Calgary Exhibition and the subsequent development of both is a testament to the enduring strength of Weadick's vision. If you asked visitors to Calgary or even Alberta to name the defining feature of the province, I suspect many would say the Stampede. There's nothing wrong with this, but I wonder if we are missing an opportunity to forge a new vision of life here – a vision that doesn't abandon our cowboy roots, but extends them to reflect our position as a global energy superpower.

Lest anyone think this new vision is already in place, what I have in mind is quite different from the current government strategy of expanding oil sands production and putting a "for sale" sign out front. I can applaud the research and industry engagement during the last two decades of the 20th century that catalyzed initial investment in the oil sands, but that was then, what about now? If we want to have economic options in 10 or 20 years, we have to begin thinking now; we can't wait until the resource is gone, the environment trashed, or our competitors have migrated to something new and better. And so it is that I lament the lobbying efforts in Ottawa and Washington by the Alberta Government. Where is the vision, the story that fires people's imaginations, the leadership?

I'm under no illusions; I know that oil and gas will remain our primary energy sources for years to come. And reliability and security of supply are indeed important, but unless we begin to write a new story about new sources of energy and new sources of wealth, we are destined to spend our capital like a drunken sailor and leave nothing for those who come after us. And the worst of it is that we have the wherewithal to forge a destiny that is genuinely exciting and captivating.

And so it is that Calgarians shouldn't allow the current oil boom to dull our senses. After all, we've been down this road before. If anything, our memory should spur us to get involved and ensure that we use today's riches to deliberately do things differently than before, better than before. To forge a truly just city; a city that is admired less for the wealth it creates than the ways in which the wealth is shared.

The happy news is that Calgary is a living laboratory for the kind of engagement Saul and Clarke - and I - want to see. Over 18,000 citizens participated in Imagine Calgary, a City-led, community-owned initiative to create a 100-year sustainability vision for Calgary, making it one of the most successful citizen engagement efforts of any city in the world. And a worthy example of ordinary people - not just NGOs and government - choosing to get involved in shaping their city. LaFontaine and Baldwin – and Guy Weadick – would be proud.

IMAGINE CALGARY: A STRATEGIC LENS TO VIEW THE FUTURE[3]

As regular viewers of the award-winning American television program, *The West Wing* (or keen students of political theory) can attest, democracy isn't easy; you have to want it bad. Put another way, the bedrock of democracy is citizen participation in the functioning, planning and decision-making of society. I've been reminded of this over the past several months as Imagine Calgary has been debated in these pages (see for example, the June 15 editorial, Imagine a city unlike any other).

It's easy to see why some might arch an eyebrow at the very idea of something like Imagine Calgary. It is, after all, popularly (if improperly) viewed as little more than "another" planning exercise and what most people really want is action. Others might note that the majority of plans and strategies fail, or fail to have the impact they might because they can't be effectively implemented. Still others will carp that it is about sustainability, that most vexing of terms, and any effort to make Calgary sustainable will inevitably stifle the entrepreneurial verve that distinguishes this place.

While it is right to note that the proof of any planning effort lies in the extent to which vision and idea are translated into on-the-ground change, it is equally right to note that not all approaches to planning are the same. And it is here that Imagine Calgary boldly stakes out new ground.

Most strategic planning efforts lack an effective process to involve the front-line people ultimately responsible for implementation. Imagine Calgary breaks from this mould in at least four ways:

- It is engaging up to 100,000 members of the public in conversations about the future of the city over a 100-year time period;
- It has created a round table and series of working groups, comprising community leaders and organizations with a mandate to implement change, to backstop the broad community engagement effort;

[3] This Op-Ed ran in the Calgary Herald on October 6, 2005. It has been revised for this publication

- It has forged productive working relationships with a variety of experts and other interested people from Calgary and elsewhere to provide periodic "reality checks" on the process; and most crucially
- It has created a mayor's panel comprising community leaders who can ensure the good ideas are translated into actions that resonate with and motivate members of the public – the panel is a tangible demonstration that there is a will to make the vision happen.

The challenge facing virtually every city today, especially one growing as fast as Calgary, is the tendency to focus on individual symptoms of non-sustainability rather than a systems-based view of the whole. Imagine Calgary holds considerable promise as a framework to guide planning and decision-making – it really is most properly viewed as a strategic lens through which economic, social and environmental challenges are viewed as interdependent parts of the same system. Such a framework also makes for more thoughtful consideration of tradeoffs.

Think of it this way: the decisions Calgary makes today about buildings and infrastructure will define the environmental impact and cost profiles for energy, water, waste, air quality, health, and many other issues within the city for the next 100 years. Infrastructure pipes, roads and subdivision layouts are typically sized and built for 100-year timelines and pay little attention to sustainability. This must change. If we learned anything from watching the devastation of New Orleans by hurricane Katrina, it was the need to ask questions about the resilience of municipal infrastructure.

Marcel Proust observed that the real act of discovery is not in finding new lands, but seeing with new eyes. Imagine Calgary represents a rare opportunity for the people of Calgary to do just this – to see their city as they perhaps haven't seen it before, to draw a picture of what they want.

Can Calgary maintain or enhance environmental quality while remaining an economic engine, and if so, how? Can it provide meaningful work for the people who live here? Can it be a place that incubates and supports new ideas in business, the arts, health and wellness, and citizen engagement? These and other questions lie at the heart of any meaningful conversation about what might make Calgary more vibrant and livable now and in the future. Imagine Calgary provides a seat at the table of that conversation for every Calgarian. Better still, it provides an opportunity for individuals and groups to shape the conversation, own a piece of the action, and see themselves as profound culture-shifting agents. Now, that is anything but the same old planning.

Down to Zero: Waste Reduction and the Art of the Possible

Introduction and Context

Thank you for those kind words of introduction. It's great to be with you this morning to share ideas in the shadow of the mountains that frame Sun Peaks Resort – an inspiring stage on which to have a conversation about something that matters. The opportunity to speak to you also represents something of a return to my professional roots, in a sense. More years ago than I care to mention, I helped to establish a used oil recovery program here in B.C. – my small contribution to the zero waste cause, if you will. More seriously, I think it's possible, perhaps even necessary, to divine a true line that links the province's work from as far back as *The Litter Act* in 1970 to Pollution Prevention Planning and Extended Producer Responsibility to the current provincial goal of leading the world in sustainable environmental management. I'll return to that lofty goal later in my remarks.

The American scholar, John Schaar, has described the future in a way that frames much of what I want to share with you this morning. He said:

> The future is not a result of choices among alternative paths offered by the present, but a place that is created – created first in mind and will, created next in activity. The future is not some place we are going to, but one we are creating. The paths are not to be found, but made, and the activity of making them, changes both the maker and the destination.

I like those words; I draw inspiration from those words, because they remind me that I have an opportunity, perhaps even an obligation, to create something, as opposed to simply reacting to what is presented to me. And the act of creating requires courage – courage to use both the head and the heart to identify possibilities, to divine new ways of being. Hence the title of my remarks this morning, "Down to Zero: Waste Reduction and the Art of the Possible".

There are times when I lament that in our quest for zero waste, we have kept our eyes too squarely focused on the ball and perhaps lost sight of the game, or more accurately, the passage of the ball through time. What I mean by that is that we are preoccupied with transactional performance (doing things right) rather than transformational performance (doing the right things). And so it is that we become incredibly good doing things that don't necessarily create the future we want. We become slaves to process and lose sight of the outcome. Don't get me wrong, waste reduction and its cousin, pollution prevention, are good, even important things to do, especially when the average Canadian sends over 300 kilograms of waste to landfills and incinerators each year, but what is the larger story of which they are a part? And how does RCBC and its supporters connect to and shape that story? Put another way, what does RCBC do in a world without waste?

An important part of this conference is celebration, and rightly so, but I think an equal measure of reflection and renewal is also good. I want to challenge you this morning, invite you, to raise the height of your radar and think about the journey to zero waste in new ways. My comments are intended to highlight those aspects of our collective thinking on "waste" that should be celebrated, loudly and proudly, but equally, to shed light on opportunities that have heretofore been overlooked. There are three dimensions to my remarks:

- Waste as it is popularly viewed by the environmental community and the general public
- Waste in a broader management context
- Waste reduction as a driver of social and organizational change.

Waste as it is Popularly Viewed by the Environmental Community and the General Public

What is this thing called waste, and why do we care about it, or getting rid of it? Well, waste as it is popularly, or perhaps I should say traditionally, viewed by the environmental community and the general public is any material with no inherent value or usefulness. There's a story unfolding in my newly adopted home of Calgary that speaks to this particular view of waste.

Last October, City Council approved the idea of a curbside recycling program to serve single-family homes. That's right, despite many outstanding features, Calgary doesn't yet have curbside recycling – unless you count the well-intentioned but limited efforts of a few private suppliers. Now, apart from the inevitable carping about costs ($24 million a year is the current estimate), and timing (pickups would start in 2009), the focus of this story is glass, newspaper, plastics, packaging and organic materials – the stuff of everyday life in a single-family household. THIS is what most people see, smell, touch and otherwise experience when they think about waste. Chris Turner's lucid description of "e-waste" in the current issue of Canadian Geographic reminds me that I should probably add those ubiquitous airplane headphones to the list, but you get the idea. The business or industrial analogue is construction and demolition debris, metals, liquid and hazardous industrial waste. And none of this is particularly exciting or interesting. Or is it? What would our world be like if these things were no longer waste? What if we had solved this particular waste "problem"? The answers to these questions represent the first layer of possibility; the base of a metaphorical waste pyramid in which we reconsider the resource intensity of our lives, and strategically reduce or remove some of the "waste".

Imagine a world with no landfills or incinerators. No transfer stations. No trucks driving to transfer stations. Better still, imagine a world in which new economic opportunity is fueled by resources previously deemed waste. The infrastructure to support such a world would be different, by design, and the ways in which we live, the ways in which we satisfy our needs and wants, would similarly be different because we would make different choices, particularly with respect to consumption. We're a long way from such a world. Which means there is room for creativity, room for ambitious, if not audacious thinking and doing. Room for a more expansive articulation and application of eco-efficiency. Whether it be process optimization or waste recycling; eco-innovation or the creation of new services, I passionately believe we can create an exciting new future, a future of access and opportunity. And you don't have to look far afield, or have especially deep pockets to get inspired.

Mountain Equipment Co-op has generated savings of $63,000 a year at its Vancouver store through recycling; Telus has saved nearly $400,000 a year through waste reduction and recycling efforts, and created a new multi-million dollar revenue stream through equipment re-sale; and in Victoria, the Dockside Green development intends to have the lightest ecological footprint of any development in the world. Also in Victoria, Level Ground Trading, the fair trade coffee importer, has adopted a "nearly zero" waste policy and used it to drive a 90% reduction in landfill waste, with consequent financial benefits. As company co-founder, Stacey Toews, put it in an interview last fall, "we have reduced landfill waste to a single grocery bag per week...only four months ago we were filling a dumpster every thirty days." Finally, the Elk Falls pulp mill on Vancouver Island, a major player in the local economy and a place my father worked for many years, retrofitted its main power boiler, and reduced landfill costs due to a significant reduction in fly ash. Maintenance costs were also reduced, which increased the boiler's availability, and reduced the mill's reliance on other energy sources. An especially important part of the Elk Falls story is the willingness of management to use a modified accounting analysis to more clearly understand the costs and benefits which shape the bottom line . The analysis included landfill costs to be sure, but also included boiler operation and maintenance, and environmental permitting costs. The results pointed to future savings that were more than double the capital cost of $10 million.

Best news of all? The companies I've named represent just the tip of a pretty big iceberg. And let's not forget the EPR successes to date, which include an 80+% recovery rate on beverage containers and used oil. There's something good happening here in B.C. More and more businesses and households see that green can be the color of money.

When I think of these case examples, the key message that lingers, apart from the flush of cost savings, is the extent to which new techniques, new skills, and new perspectives were brought to bear on the problem of improving environmental quality as well as social and economic opportunity. And so it is that P2 creates efficiencies that improve the bottom line, and EPR redefines the relationship between government, industry, local communities and the public with respect to waste management. This latter story is important; British Columbia had the strategic foresight to recognize that product manufacturers and brand owners are in the best position to reduce lifecycle environmental and health costs. Today the province has the most comprehensive list of products subject to a stewardship program of any state or province in North America. Equally important, the province is getting the prices of goods to more accurately reflect their true lifecycle costs. This is huge. In the current edition of *Report on Business magazine*, Fabrice Taylor underscores the importance of moving to a better form of lifecycle accounting. He says:

> There is a market-based fix to our predicament: If we could find a way to properly account for the full financial cost of our addiction to oil, gas and coal, the invisible hand would adjust prices and demand accordingly. So forget the tree-hugging activists; it's up to the accountants to save us from ourselves.

He's right, of course. We need to make the accounting for lifecycle costs not a novelty, not something to be showcased in a speech like this, but the norm. Notwithstanding some progress by the Canadian Institute of Chartered Accountants, we need to hold the accounting profession's feet to the fire, celebrate the willingness of managers like those at Elk Falls mill to do something different, and find more good stories to keep us moving toward a day when NOT accounting for life cycle or total costs is an attention grabber. We know this doesn't have to hurt; we know that this can be good for the environment and the bottom line.

The question now, and I appreciate that it's a question that will be debated over the next two days, is "what comes next?" How do we build from this exciting base of the pyramid and more fully articulate a world in which waste is food, fuel and opportunity?

Waste in a Broader Management Context

In 1969 Ian McHarg published *Design with Nature*, arguably the most influential book in landscape architecture and design in the 20th century, and a book that introduced many ideas that would be popularized thirty years later under the biomimicry and green chemistry labels. He begins with the words "The world is a glorious bounty". What he means is that the answers to our design (and other) questions are inevitably to be found in nature. He says:

> In the quest for survival, success and fulfillment, the ecological view offers an invaluable insight. It shows the way for [humanity to be]...steward, enhancing the creative fit of man-environment, realizing design with nature.

This is a useful touchstone for us, I think. Waste is, after all, a human construct: in nature there is no waste.

If we shift our focus from attacking specific elements of the waste stream to looking higher up on the face of the pyramid, we confront another, deeper definition of waste, "any useless or profitless activity". This definition opens up several interesting and arguably more expansive possibilities, possibilities that draw inspiration from nature, possibilities that speak to changes in entire industrial or organizational ecosystems. This definition has, for example, spurred the lean manufacturing model.

Lean is fundamentally about working with less waste, but waste is here defined in broader terms than simply materials. By adopting a lean philosophy manufacturers review all business practices in an effort to reduce all forms of waste – time, people, materials of all stripes, and so on. What's more, this review process never stops; the underlying philosophy is that no matter how good a process or practice, it can always be improved.

The Toyota Motor Company is a wonderful exemplar of this philosophy. For years the company has used "JIDOKA", automated machines with humanlike intelligence to "mistake proof" the manufacturing process. This is now found in almost every industrial enterprise, helping to reduce waste while conserving resources. More generally, Toyota has long been a proponent of "KAIZEN", an overarching business strategy rooted in sustained continuous improvement. In particular, it means a serious commitment to eliminating waste. And so it is that Toyota has adopted a vision of the future rooted in the idea of "creating a better society," and with a view toward what society is expected to be like in the medium to long term. This vision sets a course for the many roles to be played by the company vis-à-vis society, people and the planet. What's particularly germane to our discussions here is Toyota's commitment to step up and demonstrate a certain degree of responsibility as a world leader in business; and to benefit society through the creation of value-added products. This is manifesting itself in a move within the company to become a leader in what it calls "regenerative capitalism", capitalism that is good for the planet, capitalism that fosters a "recycling society" rather than a mass production/mass consumption society.

There is a subtle, but critical shift in thinking that is required if a KAIZEN-style approach to waste reduction is going to work. Instead of focusing on individual wastes, or even broad environmental aspirations, it is necessary to step further back and ask two questions: The first is "what are our overarching business or organizational objectives?" The second is "how do our efforts at waste reduction, especially the strategic choice to move toward zero waste, support or otherwise contribute to those objectives?" There's an example of a business not far from here that has asked, and continues to ask those questions.

Tolko Industries Ltd., a privately owned forest products company, operates a plywood mill in Heffley Creek. Last year, the company entered into an agreement with Nexterra Energy, a Vancouver-based company that builds gasification systems that convert solid "waste" into clean, low cost heat and power. Under the agreement, Nexterra has been building a gasification system that will convert 25,000 tonnes per year of green, bark wood residue produced on-site into clean, renewable thermal energy. The energy produced will displace approximately 235,000 gigajoules per year of natural gas currently used at the mill to produce hot water for log conditioning and to dry veneer.

It's estimated that Tolko will realize fuel cost savings of over $1.5 million annually, reduce VOC emissions from the mill, and reduce Tolko's greenhouse gas emissions by an estimated 12,000 tonnes per year. Tolko management rightly view this venture as a strategic investment in new technology that will help the company become more competitive and energy efficient.

Similarly, on May 19 General Electric, the largest company in America, and if measured by market capitalization, the largest company in the world, released its 2005 ecomagination report, showing that revenues from the sale of energy efficient and environmentally advanced products and services such as the evolution series locomotive, water reuse systems and energy star lighting hit $10.1 billion in 2005, up from $6.2 billion the year before. As GE Chairman and CEO, Jeff Immelt put it:

> Ecomagination is paying off for our investors and customers. Our advanced environmental products and services are helping customers increase their energy efficiency and reduce costs and emissions. ??

Launched just one year ago, ecomagination is GE's commitment to imagine and build innovative technologies that help customers address their environmental and financial needs. Quite apart from the obvious financial results, further proof that green is the color of money, I find the early work on ecomagination interesting because GE is using it as a platform to improve the energy efficiency of its own operations, helping to lower costs. Put another way, it is using ecomagination as a core plank of a broad competitive strategy grounded in the relentless elimination of waste and the improvement of resource intensity. The ecomagination report, Taking on Big Challenges, details GE's progress in this regard. Highlights include:

- Doubling its investment in clean research and development – GE invested $700 million in clean technologies in 2005; and
- Reducing its greenhouse gas (GHG) emissions and improving the energy efficiency of its operations – GHG intensity was reduced 10% and energy intensity was reduced 11%.

Beyond these works in progress, GE has several clean or eco technologies in its R&D pipeline, such as photovoltaics, biofuels, transportation initiatives with even higher emissions and fuel efficiency standards, and an offshore wind turbine project with the U.S. Department of Energy. Not all of these will work, or be commercially viable in the short run, and some of them never will, and in part that's why I like what GE is doing. The company has deliberately chosen to create a new future, where the rules have yet to be written. In the business vernacular of today, this is called a blue ocean strategy, a choice to leave the cutthroat competition of the known market space (the red ocean) for markets that no one else thinks about or sees. In our journey toward zero waste, in our journey up my metaphorical pyramid, and most certainly in British Columbia's journey to world-leading sustainable environmental management, we need to think more about blue ocean strategy.

Before leaving this second layer of possibility in waste reduction, I want to talk briefly about industrial ecology. My reasons are twofold. I want to tie my remarks back to Ian McHarg. And I want to explore the question of whether zero waste is always in the public interest?

Several years ago, Michael Porter, the Harvard professor and arguably the world's greatest authority on competitive strategy, and Dan Esty of Yale University examined the extent to which industrial ecology could convey competitive advantage at the level of the individual firm . Time doesn't permit a full discussion of their work, but I find their conclusions a useful caution on those of us who might otherwise promise too much, too soon in the drive to zero waste, thereby inadvertently losing credibility. Porter and Esty concluded that:

> "...industrial ecology will often be useful for firms seeking to improve their resource productivity and thus their competitiveness. The systems perspective that industrial ecology promotes can help companies find ways to add value or reduce costs both within their own production processes and up and down the supply chain. But industrial ecology cannot always be counted upon to yield competitive advantage at the firm level. In some cases, the cost of closing loops will exceed the benefits".

The authors further conclude that:

> "...because industrial ecology focuses attention on materials and energy flows, it may not optimize other variables that contribute to competitiveness within the corporate setting".

I am perhaps stating the obvious, but it seems to me that as we look for more sophisticated and nuanced approaches to waste reduction, particularly as part of a broader sustainable environmental management objective, we need to foster a way of thinking, as well as the requisite tools, that allows us to consider multiple variables that affect organizational performance. We are then better positioned to frame waste in a broader management context, and open up the even more exciting proposition of waste reduction as a driver of social and organizational change. At a firm level, this means understanding that when you make an environmental intervention, the rest of the company's activities, notably marketing and R&D, don't stop. Within government, this means bringing cabinet and ministerial colleagues onside – we have to stop preaching, generally, but especially to the converted, and listen to what others want to achieve. We then have to create or co-create the conditions where we can collaborate in the fullest and truest sense of that word.

Waste Reduction as a Driver of Social and Organizational Change

What happens as you reach the top of the waste pyramid? Is it possible to think of waste reduction as something that might actually drive social and organizational change? A recent article in *The Calgary Herald* sheds some light on this question. The article, in the business section, profiled Internet pioneers who are placing strategic bets on the "net big thing".

Two decades ago people like Steve Case (America on Line founder) and Bill Gates (co-founder of Microsoft) saw the Internet as a way to make money and change the world. Today, they think green technology is poised to make a similar impact. John Doerr, a venture capitalist who invested early in Google and Amazon, recently set up a $100 million fund to invest in "green technology", something he believes could be the largest economic opportunity of the 21st century. As Case put it in an interview published in *The Washington Post*, "the green movement is going mainstream and we want to ride that wave".

Now, some of you might think this is a bit of a stretch, but there are some real parallels between clean technology and the early days of the Internet. Chief among them is the fact that clean tech is starting from a relatively small base, it's being driven by radical innovation, and it's underinvested relative to the size of the potential market.

In this room today we have the hearts and minds necessary to ignite a pretty exciting conversation about where and how clean technology, RCBC and its supporters, and the journey to zero waste come together. Equally, we have the wherewithal to talk about paradigm-busting ideas that lead not to "best in class performance", but to breakaway strategies that put you in a class of your own. I encourage all of you to spark these kinds of conversations. As inspiration, I think of TerraCycle, a small and energetic new company, founded by a Canadian, that produces the world's first consumer product line that is both made from waste and packaged in waste.

The product is plant food, derived from organic waste, and the packaging is used pop bottles. The bottles are collected through school fundraising drives across the US and Canada. In this way, the company has found a novel way of sourcing a key raw material, and inspiring students to actively engage with their communities. These bottles are stripped, cleaned, and filled directly with TerraCycle Plant Food. This past year, over 250,000 bottles were collected - many of which ended up on the shelves of Home Depot, Loblaws, and Whole Foods, to name a few. Last summer TerraCycle set a record for the fastest selling plant food in a Home Depot Website test.

In hindsight our vision is always acute, but come on, here's a successful new business based on producing an environmentally friendly product from garbage packaged in recycled bottles. I believe we can learn a lot from TerraCycle as we seek to answer the "what comes next" question and move closer to the promised land of zero waste.

The Ford Motor Company's Rouge River facility in Dearborn,

Michigan is also an interesting example of what can be done as one moves closer to the top of the waste pyramid. The plant supports a cycle-to-cycle protocol, where waste is continually fed into the system as a food source. The company, much in the news of late for poor (some would say junk bond status) performance, has nonetheless done us all a service by developing the prototype car, Model U, a cycle-to-cycle vehicle whose materials can go back to the soil, or back to industry.

Inspired by how the Model T revolutionized personal transportation at the beginning of the 20th century, Ford has invested a good deal of creative thought, and no small amount of money, in Model U. One might well make the case that 100 years ago the Model T offered the most advanced manufacturing and was built with the most advanced materials. What we might see with Model U is an echo of that design philosophy – updated to reflect contemporary aspirations.

It is premature to say that the Model U starts a new era of low or no emissions, radically advanced safety and fuel economy, and not simply green materials and processes, but ecologically restorative materials and processes. It is also not clear if Ford's current financial crisis will overshadow and ultimately eclipse the Model U, or if the car and the thinking it reflects will light the way ahead for the company. Still, the thinking it represents about how the essential human need for mobility might be addressed in a zero waste way is exciting and might well be a blueprint for a host of radical design concepts in the future.

The Herman Miller furniture company also serves as a compass in navigating towards zero waste in new and nuanced ways. The company has just released its first cradle-to-cradle, non-PVC chair. This is a fitting tribute to the company's founder, D.J. DePree, who as early as 1936 saw a moral dimension to the design of furniture. The company's cultural ethos is one of concern for the larger issues of humanity and equality and bettering the world we work in. Visit the company's web site and you will read one of the best statements of what it means to be a mission-driven organization:

What arrives on the truck is furniture. What went into the truck was an amalgam of what we believe in: innovation, design, operational excellence, smart application of technology, and social responsibility.

I also believe we can learn from a much larger example, an example of what I will call the recycling ethos applied to landscape design. The Eden Project near Cornwall, England arouses the senses and dramatically shows how human civilization relies on plants. What has this got to do with waste, you ask? Well, the project was built into and around a 200-foot-deep disused china clay pit. It is a remarkable, and remarkably creative response to several issues that strike at the heart of sustainability – how to create economic opportunity in a depressed region; how to address post-mine closure in a new and exciting way; and how to engage and educate people on the interdependence between humans and the natural world.

Since opening in 2001, Eden, as it is popularly known, has become England's leading tourist attraction. Indeed, even before it was completed, the project had the distinction of being the most visited construction site in the world.

In many respects, the examples of TerraCycle, Ford, Herman Miller and Eden are wonderful illustrations of Proust's assertion that the real act of discovery lies not in visiting new lands, but in seeing with new eyes. They are also living proof of Bruce Mau's Massive Change project, namely:

> The new design model provides a continuous assembly / disassembly line that cycles the product and its constituent matter in a never-ending loop of improvement.

There is one final story, one final example I want to share with you.

In a speech toward the end of 2005, Ray Anderson, the charismatic Chairman of Interface (and a member of the David Suzuki Foundation Board) highlighted three aspects of his company's journey to sustainability that I find compelling and highly relevant to our deliberations here. The cumulative savings from eliminating waste in the manufacturing process have been $289 million over 10 years – that's nearly $30 million of found money each year, and a pretty potent retort to the charge that sustainability costs money. Perhaps more impressive, he says that Interface's products are the best they've ever been because sustainability has proven to be an unimagined source of inspiration and innovation – his people are galvanized around a higher purpose. This is the conversation I'd like you to have – we're all good at "transactional" work, executing the game plan; but are we missing the much more exciting game of "transformational" work? This idea of a higher purpose, is really about self-actualization. And you can't beat it for bringing people together and rounding out the business case. As Anderson puts it, "there is no amount of money we could have spent on advertising that would have generated as much goodwill or contributed as much to the top line, to winning business. To those of you who have the occasional "dark night of the soul" and wonder why we're doing this work, or how we can convince others, there's your answer.

Concluding Thoughts and Closing poem by David Whyte

In closing, I'd like to return to the current provincial objective, one of the so-called "five great goals", of leading the world in sustainable environmental management. So of course I need to say something about leadership.

Leadership is about innovation. It's about asking what needs to be done and why. It's about taking a deliberately long-term view. In many respects I think British Columbia can take pride in its environmental performance and talk confidently about leadership. *The Litter Act* in 1970 was a leadership decision. The decisions of the early 1990s on product stewardship, and the launch of pollution prevention planning in the mid-1990s were leadership decisions. I especially remember the language from the province's document, Introduction to Pollution Prevention Planning for Major Industrial Operations:

> "...today, both government and industry recognize that it is necessary to move up the pipe to avoid, eliminate and reduce pollution at its source...Pollution prevention also provides value-added benefits to industry. It is as much about increasing efficiency, reducing costs, improving flexibility and gaining a competitive advantage as it is about enhancing the ability to protect the environment."

There is probably a lifetime of work in those words. And it's the best kind of work; the kind of work that makes you want to do more than simply show up. Those words excite me; they make me want to do the very best work that I can do. They also make me want to ask, "Okay, where are we now, what comes next, what needs to be done?" And I'm moved to ask those questions because the people of British Columbia, the constituents we serve, want us to ask those questions. British Columbians have recognized for some time that sustainability of their economy and communities is dependent on preservation of a sustainable environment.

My friends, we need to keep raising the bar, we need to keep asking what comes next? What is the good work that we need to be doing now?

In part, this means taking a closer look at the goal of leading the world in sustainable environmental management and contributing to what I hope can become an ongoing strategic conversation about what that goal means. If we have the best air and water quality, and the best fisheries management, the current meaning of the expression, does that cut it? I would suggest that it does not, but I also appreciate that you've got to start somewhere. It means understanding where we currently sit with respect to performance, and becoming ever more creative in improving performance. This is where the principles and practice of ecological design can help us – we can systematically think or re-think a product or service to minimize the impact of materials and manufacturing, to optimize distribution, to make its use have a light footprint on the earth and society, to optimize the lifetime of the product or service, as well as the end-of-life. This is also where initiative such as Our Future in the Balance, an event in Vancouver early last month that profiled waste reduction and sustainability projects in B.C. schools, and the upcoming Waste Reduction Week in October, and so many others, are useful arrows in our quiver. But it seems to me that as good and useful as these things are, we need more, we need better, and we need different.

We need to embrace what Joanna Macy calls The Great Turning, the essential work of our time, the shift from an industrial growth society to a life sustaining civilization.

We're beginning to do this. We're taking action to slow the damage to the Earth and its peoples, at least in an ad hoc way. And we're even beginning to address the structural causes of our global sustainability crisis – the tacit agreements between individuals, governments, businesses and civil society organizations that define "the way things are done". Equally, we are beginning to propose alternative structural models. Where we have much work to do is in shifting the consciousness of everyone who is traveling with us on Spaceship Earth. As we articulate structural alternatives that redefine our relationship with the earth and with each other, we need to acknowledge that this is the stuff of cognitive revolution and spiritual awakening. We need to step back from what is right in front of us and say that the answers to what most ails us are likely to be found in deep ecology, spiritual traditions, especially indigenous spiritual traditions, eco-feminism, and eco-psychology – *and the integration of these ways of knowing.* And so, whether it is RCBC looking forward 5 years, the government re-thinking one of its 5 great goals, or one of you thinking about what comes next in your personal or professional life, I encourage – no that's not strong enough – I exhort you to embrace The Great Turning. It will help you climb my metaphorical waste pyramid, but it will do so much more than that.

As a motivational bridge that might help you begin this work, I want to share an excerpt from a poem by David Whyte that has always helped to both ground me, and exhilarate me. The poem is called *What to Remember When Waking:*

> You are not a troubled guest on this earth,
> you are not an accident amidst other accidents
> you were invited from another and greater night than the one
> from which you have just emerged.
> Now, looking through the slanting light of the morning
> window toward the mountain presence of everything that can
> be, what urgency calls you to your one love? What shape
> waits in the seed of you to grow and spread its branches
> against a future sky?

Think of those good words as you listen to other speakers, and to each other, over the next 2 days. Use them as a talisman against the safe, the routine, the transactional. Use them to help ignite transformation.

Bridging the Gap between Strategy and Sustainability[5]

The American lawyer and legal historian, William Jennings Bryan, famously observed that "destiny is not a matter of chance, it is a matter of choice; it is not a thing to be waited for, it is a thing to be achieved." I think of those good words whenever someone asks me what is needed to accelerate the transition to sustainability, especially among businesses. The answer lies in bridging the gap between strategy and sustainability.

In the past decade there has been impressive work undertaken by many businesses around the world under the auspices of sustainability. While this work is to be celebrated, it should also be placed in context in at least two ways.

First, environmental or erstwhile sustainability departments have largely led it; other key resources, notably finance and operations, have not been actively or consistently involved. As a result, we have an interesting portfolio of projects across several companies and industries, but we have yet to see true organizational transformation as a result of a deeply embedded commitment to sustainability. Put another way, sustainability isn't yet part of the organizational DNA in a critical mass of companies.

Second, the state of our planet has become more perilous, not less. The *Millennium Ecosystem Assessment*, the most comprehensive study of critical ecosystem goods and services yet undertaken, reported that human actions are depleting Earth's natural capital and putting such strain on the environment that the ability of the planet's ecosystem to sustain future generations can no longer be taken for granted. As the most influential agent in society, business has an opportunity to lead the charge to a more sustainable society.

Here's how.

Pragmatic business

Job #1 is to define our terms properly. Sustainability – the dynamic interplay of economic, social and environmental aspirations – is not ideological; it's a pragmatic response to hard core business realities

[5] First published in *Green Business Magazine* in January of 2008 and revised for this publication.

that are cast into sharp relief by strategic planning and risk assessment that looks beyond the horizon of the next quarter or the next year. There is a reason beyond altruism that explains why several large institutional investors now routinely demand an assessment of climate change risk prior to investing in a company. Similarly, when Duke Energy's chief strategist said earlier this year that his company had a duty to its shareholders to spend more than $15 billion over the next decade to drive down GHG emissions, he wasn't talking about corporate philanthropy; he was talking about long-term risk management.

Alfred Chandler, in his classic text, Strategy and Structure, defined strategy as:

> ...the determination of the basic long-term goals and objectives of an enterprise, and the adoption of courses of action and the allocation of resources necessary for carrying out these goals.

Anyone who doesn't think sustainability and corporate responsibility will shape the choice of actions and the allocation of resources is placing their organization at a competitive disadvantage. More charitably, companies that treat sustainability solely as an environmental or corporate social responsibility issue, rather than a strategic business issue, will expose themselves to risk – and miss new opportunities. We must set ideology aside and treat the creation of wealth and well being in an era of heightened concern for the quality of the natural and social environment – the essence of the sustainability challenge – as the latest point on the evolutionary curve of business strategy.

Consider this question. What percentage of your firm's profits is reinvested in an innovation agenda aimed at reducing your environmental footprint; reducing your overall carbon risk; and/or accelerating your company's transition to sustainability? Your answer will go a long way toward determining if you are bridging the gap between strategy and sustainability.

Full engagement

Job #2 is to define the size of the prize. For example, do you know what your financial exposure is as a result of greenhouse gas emissions? I recently did a simple comparison of reported net income versus GHG emissions for some of Canada's largest companies. Even at a conservative carbon price of $15 per tonne, the price tag these companies might face if forced to reduce emissions (or pay into a technology fund) ranged from one to nine per cent of income.

More broadly, can you envision sustainability as an unimagined source of inspiration and innovation for your employees and other stakeholders – something that galvanizes your people around a higher purpose? Can you imagine saying that there is no amount of money you could spend on advertising that would generate as much goodwill, or contribute as much to the reputation of your company as your response to the sustainability challenge?

This requires a fundamental reframing of sustainability as something that transcends the domain of the VP of sustainability, the manager of environmental affairs, or the director of community investment – the CEO, COO and CFO need to be actively engaged. This is about sustainability as a strategic opportunity to build a great business.

Bridge building

Job #3 is to build bridges in the community towards a more sustainable business future. This requires that the business community think beyond next-quarter financial results, to be sure, but it also requires that sustainability advocates develop a deeper appreciation for how business strategy is created and implemented.

How does a company decide what it wants to be, what it wants to do? Does it want to shape the industry of which it is a part; adapt to opportunities as they present themselves; or reserve the right to play under several possible scenarios by making incremental investments? The answers to these questions are important – they will define the particular sources of advantage around which the company builds its strategy. Every action that is taken, every effort to create value, flows from this decision.

As advocates for sustainability, we must understand, or better still, contribute to the creation of this strategic map and demonstrate where and how sustainability supports broad strategy. And of course, understanding this map not only gives us more influence over risks and opportunities, but also allows us to create value for shareholders and, perhaps, more importantly, for society as a whole.

WHY CLIMATE CHANGE IS A STRATEGIC BUSINESS ISSUE[6]

The emergence of climate change as perhaps the defining challenge of our time has sharpened the debate over how best to reconcile economic development with environmental protection and social welfare. A rapidly expanding body of evidence, coupled with timely media coverage, has moved climate change from a largely scientific debate to a global consensus that: human activity is exacerbating natural variation in climate, and something must be done to curb the human imprint on climate.

Reducing human reliance on fossil fuels, and the GHG emissions associated with their use, is seen as an essential first step. This creates risk for virtually every business and elevates climate change to a strategic and operational imperative. For example, late in 2007 two environmental NGOs in the US, joined by state and city financial officers, petitioned the US Securities and Exchange Commission to require companies to reveal their financial exposure to climate change risks. Further, the State of Florida recently moved to require managers of the $20 billion treasury fund to account for climate change risk in all of their investments. As Brian Storms, President and CEO of Marsh, put it in what can now be seen as a prescient February 2006 conference call with the firm's 30,000 corporate clients:

> Climate change is probably one of the best examples of where long-term risk planning is essential to mitigate some potentially irreversible long-term effects.

While the nature and pace of change – in regulations, consumer tastes and preferences, capital markets and technology – is unclear, it seems inevitable that the day is not far off when all companies' GHG emissions will be measured, regulated, and priced.

Understanding the risk universe

There are five key risks associated with climate change that merit C-suite attention: (1) financial; (2) reputation; (3) competitiveness;

---

[6] First published in *Green Business Magazine* in March of 2008 and revised for this publication

(4) regulatory; and (5) litigation. From a financial perspective, shareholders and investment fund managers are increasingly asking hard questions of companies about the management of (financial) risk associated with climate change. Every CFO, COO and CEO should have a solid answer to the following:

- How many tonnes of GHG does the company currently emit – including emissions from the end use of any company products – and what steps is it taking to reduce emissions?
- What is the company doing to protect shareholder value in light of current and possible climate change regulations?

In addition, every CRO needs to understand if their company's emissions are creating financial exposure that needs to be discussed at the Board level.

It is not hard to imagine a shareholder revolt, or worse, if smart answers to these questions aren't forthcoming. After all, is it really a stretch to imagine a lawsuit rooted in the idea that a company suffered financially due to a lack of planning for climate risk? The damage to company reputation over real or perceived failure to manage an emergent issue like this – and the effect this has on recruitment and retention efforts, access to capital, cost of capital, and so on – could all be severe.

Competitively, companies that do not fully appreciate both the gains in operational effectiveness associated with reducing their carbon footprint, and the ways in which climate change will re-shape their competitive landscape, will find themselves at a competitive disadvantage if their competition sees these issues more clearly and seizes the opportunity they create. While climate change regulations have been evolving only slowly, enforcement or market action against companies that are not reducing their GHG emissions and retooling their production process is inevitable . This creates the potential for litigation, limitations on market access, and reputation damage – to cite just three of the more likely impacts.

Reframing climate risk as opportunity

The risk universe is, of course, just one side of the climate change coin.

The other side is about opportunity – opportunity for innovation that reframes and redesigns a business. This is what underlies Dell's recent decision to become the "greenest technology firm in the world" and become carbon neutral. In a January 31, 2008 report in *The Globe and Mail*, it was noted that this company has publicly stated that it believes it can appeal to more potential customers, attract more capital from environmentally and socially conscious investors, and reduce operating expenses, especially on fuel and electricity.

Dell's appointment of Gilbert Casellas, former Chairman of the US Equal Employment Opportunities Commission, as Vice-President of Corporate Responsibility in October 2007, reinforces the commitment – and strategic intent – of the company in this regard. As reported on the Dell website, Casellas and his team "will oversee the heightened integration of economic, social and environmental responsibility into everything we do".

Wal-Mart's recent market moves related to climate change are also grounded in opportunity. The company's report on sustainability progress to date notes that "if we improve our fleet fuel mileage by just 1 mile per gallon, we can save over $40 million a year". These savings contribute to a strategically virtuous circle that includes both lower prices for Wal-Mart customers as well as environmental benefits associated with reduced fuel emissions.

Is your company leaving significant money on the table by not thinking about the underlying drivers of climate risk and opportunity and taking steps to reclaim some of that money? This is, after all, about improving operational effectiveness – something that any business should strive for. And what about the other, broader question of how climate change affects the competitive landscape? Joe Stanislaw, Co-founder of Cambridge Energy Research Associates, has noted that the emergence of climate change as a topic of mainstream discussion could (and perhaps should) catalyze a new era of market-driven innovation in alternative energy, conservation, and international cooperation.

The transition to a less carbon intensive economy won't happen overnight; at least two generations are needed. The strategic rub is that many of the key decisions and investments need to be made soon. Companies that understand this and see climate change as a lens through which to view new strategic possibilities in alternative and renewable energy sources and services will be the real winners in one of the most important races humanity has ever run.

How Sustainability Helps Win the War for Talent[7]

Much has been written of late – and probably more said, concerning the so-called "war for talent", a term popularized by a 1998 McKinsey and Company report. While the rigors of recruiting and retaining employees, especially engineering, IT and management staff, do not rival those associated with real military conflict, the metaphor is still an apt one. Business is, after all, a competitive affair with winners and losers tallied in the market. Further, the rules, both explicit and implicit, governing business are undergoing great change as we complete the transition from an industrial to a post-industrial economy. Two key shifts are worthy of mention here:

- Demographic trends point to an easing of labor force growth in coming decades, making all types of workers scarce.
- The economy is changing from one in which many employees are interchangeable to one in which knowledgeable employees, charter members of the creative class, are fundamentally important to competitive success and value creation. The talent that companies need is the talent to analyze, communicate, entertain and invent – and it is becoming difficult to attract and keep employees with these critical skills.

Collectively, these shifts and the inherently competitive nature of business are creating conditions in which companies legitimately battle each other for the people that can both create and implement new ideas, products and services.

[7] First published in Green Business Magazine in September 2008 and revised for the publication.

So, how does sustainability figure in all of this?

In keeping with the general mainstreaming of sustainability in recent years, more and more job seekers are placing emphasis on sustainability (caring for employees, caring for external stakeholders, environmental stewardship, ethical business conduct) when deciding where to work – or where to keep working. With respect to this latter point, which underscores the strategic importance of retaining good people once you get them in the door, new research by Fresh Marketing points to the fact that employees have embraced sustainability and want their employers to follow suit – they want it to be okay to bring their values to work. The "2008 Corporate Sustainability Employee Study" goes a long way toward measuring the gap between employee hopes and expectations in this regard, and actual progress by employers. For example, nine out of ten employees in the survey link brand reputation with environmental and social stewardship, but 83% of employers have not yet fully incorporated corporate responsibility and sustainability performance into business metrics. This is a strategic disconnect that needs to be fixed.

With respect to the other end of the employee continuum, attracting the right talent, new work from David Montgomery at the Stanford Business School is especially enlightening. In a survey of 759 graduating MBAs at 11 top business schools, Montgomery found that future business leaders ranked corporate social responsibility high on their list of values and desired employer attributes, and backstopped that with a willingness to sacrifice up to 14% of their expected salary to find an employer whose thinking matched their own. To drive the point home, Montgomery found that a reputation for ethical conduct and caring policies towards employees ranked 75% as high as intellectual challenge and 95% as high as financial compensation.

What all of this should mean for corporate strategists is a renewed and potentially refocused positioning of sustainability within the organization. While there are many good reasons to integrate sustainability more deeply with core business strategy (easier access to capital, and at potentially less cost; better relations with regulators; access to new markets; and so on), the ability to leverage sustainability in support of workforce planning and human capital management is a rich new reward for smart companies. After all, where is next quarter's, or next year's, breakthrough products or services going to come from? In a knowledge-driven economy, these products and services come from people, working in organizations that have created the conditions that allow them to unleash their creativity and realize their full potential.

The war for talent is real, and it is being fought on many fronts. Smart companies that want to be employers of choice (and by definition, successful organizations) will gain leverage in this battle by not only doing the basics of providing solid compensation and benefits packages, but also going further to forge a corporate culture that inspires and engages, that creates space for talented people to grow, and perhaps most importantly, that models corporate responsibility and sustainability values that align with the values of their employees and new recruits. This is the human capital challenge of the next decade, but it is also more than that, it is arguably the defining strategic challenge for business – companies that navigate this challenge well will win the war for talent, and the larger battle in the market.

VALUING NATURE'S CAPITAL[8]

Although corporate responsibility has become part of the business lexicon recently, it's not a new concept. In 1915, the Canadian Commission on Conservation noted that "each generation is entitled to the interest on the natural capital, but the principal should be handed on unimpaired". If intervening generations – particularly more recent ones, including our own – had heeded this wise counsel, we might find ourselves in a different world today. Instead, we are faced with the immutable reality that our natural capital is nearing depletion.

Dana Meadows, one of the world's preeminent systems thinkers, had anticipated the urgency of this situation in a 1998 report on indicators and information systems for sustainability:

> The world economy is doubling roughly every twenty years. The world population is doubling every 40 to 50 years. The planet that supplies the materials and energy necessary for the functioning of the population and economy is not growing at all.

We do not protect what we do not value

In the past 50 years, the environment has been treated as little more than a source of raw materials to fuel economic growth and a sink to absorb wastes. Until fairly recently, two dangerous assumptions have supported this narrow view. The first is a belief that nature can supply unlimited resources (oil, fish, timber and so on) for our economic needs and fully absorb our byproducts. The second is that the availability of life-support services (breathable air, clean water, natural regulation of climate and disease, nutrient cycling, crop pollination and so on) will continue unabated despite human economic activity.

The time has come to recognize these beliefs as misconceptions: the ecosystem's resources and services are neither limitless nor "free" in economic terms. In fact, they are estimated to be worth almost twice as much as the monetary results of society's economic activities.

[8] First published in *Green Business Magazine* in May of 2008 and revised for this publication.

For example, the World Business Council for Sustainable Development notes that if a shrimp farm in Thailand was created by cutting down mangrove forests the net income from the farm would be about $8,000 per hectare. Meanwhile, the destruction of the forest and pollution from the farm would result in a loss of ecosystem services worth $35,000 per hectare. As long as prices fail to reflect the true worth of nature's "free" services, they will be squandered.

Signs of progress

There are signs of progress. We are beginning to place economic value on certain natural capital assets. Recent experience in Canada and elsewhere in pricing each tonne of CO2 emitted above a certain threshold is a good example. While early efforts to establish value for natural capital have been awkward and volatile, they indicate the strategic direction of the debate among businesses and other organizations.

The cultural landscape has been fundamentally altered, and sustainability is now a persistent issue. Particularly high on the public radar screen is climate change, due to regular illustrations of the way it can accelerate the destruction of natural capital assets. However, while climate change has spurred considerable government, corporate and NGO action, we should be under no illusions about the impact of a reduction in GHG emission intensity or the sequestration of CO2. These initiatives are only part of the broader strategic solution. A more holistic, strategic approach to sustainability is called for.

Sustainability as strategy

Corporate strategists should consider how increased public and government concern about sustainability will change their organizations' competitive context, as well as the viability of their current business models and plans. Specifically, they need to ask:

- What is my firm's exposure to the destruction or degradation of natural capital assets?
- How resilient is my firm to significant shifts in government policy directed at the protection of natural capital assets?

- What will be the impact to my firm if access to water and other key resource inputs is restricted, regulated, or otherwise made more expensive?
- What will be the impact if the price of oil rebounds from its late 2008 slide and climbs back to $100 per barrel and above?
- If my firm reclaims a disturbed site by substituting one type of habitat for the original one, does that truly limit my firm's exposure to charges that we degraded natural capital assets?

Looking ahead, at least two significant changes must occur if we are to take up the sustainability challenge in a meaningful way. First, we must shift the way we price all goods and services in the economy to more accurately reflect their true environmental and social cost. Second, we must develop a context to ensure that commerce takes place within the limits of nature. These are daunting challenges that will require the full attention and cooperation of both strategists and environmentalists. But as with all challenges, there is also opportunity. Those who move early to stake out bold positions with respect to the protection of natural capital will succeed in differentiating themselves from competitors.

IN PRAISE OF AUDACIOUS GREEN GOALS[9]

Setting the Context

In their popular 1997 book *Built to Last: Successful Habits of Visionary Companies*, Jim Collins and Jerry Porras made a persuasive argument in support of something they called the "big hairy audacious goal" or BHAG. As they saw it, a BHAG was "...an audacious 10-to-30-year goal to progress towards an envisioned future." Boeing's decision in the 1950s to build a prototype commercial jet, allowing them to leapfrog McDonnell-Douglas, and U.S. President Kennedy's call in the early 1960s to place a man on the moon within a decade are famous examples of BHAGs.

And the trend continues. It is now common to hear executives talk about doubling the size of their company, or doubling the share price, or achieving record profits. Less common, though, are executives staking out an environmental or sustainable BHAG. In view of the material and strategic significance of climate change, the transition to a low or no carbon economy would seem to be an obvious BHAG.

Instead, we have many well-intentioned but incremental efforts that fail to serve as a "unifying focal point of effort, and act as a clear catalyst for team spirit." Why? The reasons may be a tendency to focus on measures or metrics rather than the long-term viability of the strategy, and a persistent belief that environmental performance is not material to financial performance.

Pay attention to what is framed, not the frame itself

Too many organizations are preoccupied with measures or indicators (the frame) and have inadvertently lost sight of the actual strategy (what is being framed). What gets measured gets managed goes the mantra, leading managers to try and translate their organization's strategic intent into measures or indicators that can be counted, used to improve organizational decisions and performance, and reported to shareholders and other stakeholders.

---

[9] First published in *Green Business Magazine* in July of 2008 and revised for this publication.

While the need to measure is intuitively clear, a significant opportunity cost in the current emphasis on measurement is likely often overlooked – namely, failure to resist the organization's standard procedures and challenge strategies that promise only incremental or transactional change. The measures that accompany such strategies may not serve as an accurate gauge of future performance. For example, what does failing to set "audacious" goals with respect to low carbon or no carbon energy alternatives – and backstopping those goals with new types of performance measures – say about a company's forward-thinking capabilities? Is the company ceding the energy playing field of the future to innovators and start-ups few of us have yet heard of? Oil and gas companies that have made modest investments in renewable energy, for instance, could set a BHAG for renewables and partner with others through spin-offs or subsidiaries. This allows the oil and gas company to focus on what it does best, while staking a more aggressive claim or option on the probable energy sources of the future. To get there, however, company executives will have to realize that environmental excellence can drive positive financial results – now and in the future.

Connect green to the bottom line

The World Business Council for Sustainable Development (WBCSD), representing companies responsible for a significant proportion of global GDP, has demonstrated that eco-efficiency is a rock-solid business strategy that links financial and environmental performance by creating more value with less environmental impact. More companies need to know this, practice this, and use this as a platform for transformative change. Differentiation advantage – springing from a product's characteristics and performance as well as from favorable social, emotional, and psychological reactions that enhance the firm's image and reputation – may be especially important in this regard. Differentiation may also result in a firm being accorded a lower cost of capital because it is perceived to be less risky overall, and equally important, it may help companies gain access to resource plays that are closed to others. This latter feature is critically important to companies seeking social license to grow their asset base.

The elegance of eco-efficiency is that it allows business to gain traction in several different ways – from process optimization to waste recycling; from eco-innovation to the creation of new services. DuPont's record over the past decade should be both a source of inspiration to other companies who have yet to set audacious green goals, and a potent response to those who still think it doesn't pay to be green. Dupont has achieved a 91% reduction in air carcinogens; a 47% reduction in hazardous wastes; and a 68% reduction in greenhouse gas emissions from 1990 levels. Perhaps most impressively, the company has increased production by 40% with zero increase in energy use. These environmental achievements have saved DuPont an estimated $3 billion.

Jack Welch, the former CEO of General Electric, famously observed that if the world outside your business is changing faster than the world inside your business, the end is near. And it's true – the mainstreaming of sustainability in recent years represents a very fast change in the outside world for many businesses. The best response is to step away from incremental strategies and the measures that go with them, and to increase work on audacious or transformational green goals that can light the way to a new type of business, and a new type of economy.

Building a Winning Strategy for the New Economic Game

Framing the Discussion

Let's face it; people are scared right now. The economy is convulsing and there is much talk about the environment being "off the table" of policy and business decision-making as the focus shifts to job protection or the containment of losses. While the fear is real and understandable, the solution is less about expensive and incremental change through bailouts, and stimulus packages than a national economic strategy that heralds whole system change. And for all the polite talk of a "green stimulus", this sends the wrong signal – we need a 21st century economic strategy that does more than give a nod to green; we need a strategy that is smart enough to feature green throughout its underlying logic. Well intentioned but incremental thinking is akin to doing the best we can within the rules of the game. The events of the past 6 months tell us the game has changed, the ground has shifted. We need a strategy that serves us well in this new game – regardless of our vocational or political affiliation.

Context

In Robert Frost's iconic poem, *The Road Not Taken*, the narrator takes the road less travelled by. "And that has made all the difference." It is time for businesses and governments in Canada to similarly shift to a new and different road, one with which they are unfamiliar, but that can make "all the difference." As one who has worked closely with businesses and governments all over the world, I'm sympathetic to the idea that society should reward successful initiative with profit. However, as we have seen too often, especially in recent years, profit-seeking activities can have disastrous economic, social and environmental effects. And these effects, unchecked, can eat away at the foundations of civilization. This realization led John Ruskin to suggest, as the industrial revolution was still in its nascent stages a hundred and fifty years ago, that what "seems to be wealth may in verity only be the gilded index of far-reaching ruin." Ruskin coined the term "illth" to describe the side effects of an economic system that doesn't work for everyone.

I've thought about this a good deal lately because although much has been written and said about the global financial crisis, there is another, parallel crisis that also heralds the need for whole system change. In October 2008, the International Union for the Conservation of Nature (IUCN) announced that at least one-quarter of mammals worldwide are heading toward extinction – caused almost exclusively by human activity. In addition, the IUCN reported that reptiles, fish, and birds across the world are all in decline.

Answering the Call

In light of the above, I believe we need to resist the temptation to take the environment, or social justice concerns for that matter, off the table and focus solely on getting the economy moving. Such a response might staunch the bleeding, but it will do little to create the conditions for long-term health. There is another path. The combination of ecosystem decline and the global financial crisis creates a rare opportunity for the kind of whole system change we need.

Seventy years ago Joseph Schumpeter, in his influential book, *Capitalism, Socialism and Democracy*, defined profit as "the premium put upon successful innovation in capitalist society and [it] is temporary by nature: it will vanish in the subsequent process of competition and adaptation". In an era characterized by hyper-competition and uncertain economic conditions, it seems clear to me that businesses need to reinvest a portion of any profits in activities that deliberately push the envelope of their firm's business model – incremental change won't cut it. It also means governments have to get smart about innovation and macroeconomic policy. I envision a two-step process moving forward to seize the opportunity.

Seizing the Opportunity

Business has to ask some simple and yet powerful questions about where sustainability can help:

- Contain costs (by reducing waste or accelerating permit approvals, for example);
- Keep people motivated (leveraging sustainability in talent recruitment);
- Reduce exposure to costly future regulation (broaden project incentive structures from cost and schedule to include natural resource consumption or carbon risk mitigated); and
- Create economic opportunity in new, 21st century technologies

At the same time, governments have to put aside old ideas and step up to forge a new dialogue with business, academia, NGOs and other stakeholders that intentionally links innovation, R&D, and the economy with the environment and sustainability. Why can't we talk about how we meet the challenges of climate change, for example, while simultaneously securing our economic future? It is time we bridged the gap that has too long separated economic and environmental concerns in this country (and elsewhere). We can still talk about jobs, but why can't they be green jobs? And for those who have lost their jobs, I'm all for creating the conditions that support you in transitioning to something new or better. This is a strategic investment, not a knee-jerk reaction that props up an old (and beaten) business model. We can still talk about technology, but why can't that technology be in service of a 21st century economy? Most importantly, we can still talk about quality of life, but quality must increasingly be defined less by material consumption of goods and services and more by awareness of our individual and collective environmental footprint.

Forging a New Dialogue

If crisis does indeed create opportunity, I believe the winning strategy for the new economic game that is emerging lies in disenthralling ourselves from conventional wisdom, to use Lincoln's phrase, and getting on with the work of building the new economy we need – one that respects people and the environment; one that links jobs and the environment; one that reconciles radical innovation and sustainability.

Close to the Earth

In the stillness, before the day is fully awake,
I step through the garden.
Feet cushioned by wet grass.
Moist skin of the earth.
Food and flowers consecrate this place.
History written in soil.
To till this ground is to turn over stories
of those who came before.
At this hour, you perceive the world freshly, nakedly.
You feel the pulse of nature.
Snow drops and crocuses push toward the sun.
Precious warmth, life.
Beauty no longer veiled.
Apple and pear blossoms explode in color against grey wood.
Sweet fragrance too, and the promise of rich, wet fruit.
Thoreau, another early riser,
would say thought breeds thought,
it grows under your hand.
I think about contact,
My skin connected to the earth.
I think about history, ancestors
My presence here fleeting.
I think about my essence
Things that mark my passage
and speak to my love.
Of this place.

NOTES TO SECTION 4

i And of course, paying attention to stakeholders has long been a key tenet of good strategy thinking. Michael Porter's elegant and hugely influential five forces model, for example, while not conceived with sustainability as I define it here in mind, is nonetheless a powerful place to begin for many businesses. If a business understands the bargaining power of suppliers and buyers, the threat of new entrants and/or substitute products or services, and rivalry among existing firms – and how this competitive context is changing, the business can begin to deepen relationships with certain critical players (stakeholders by any other word).

ii See John Ehrenfeld's essay, "Being and Havingness" in the winter issue of Forum for Applied Research and Public Policy, 2000, pp.36-37. See also Ehrenfeld's 2008 book, Sustainability by Design: A Subversive Strategy for Transforming our Consumer Culture.

iii The LaFontaine-Baldwin lecture series is one of the most prominent lecture series on issues concerning the public good in Canada.

iv Traditional accounting methods tend to 'pool' costs into a limited number of accounts. This means that costs such as insurance, regulatory fees and maintenance, which are associated with specific outputs and activities, may be partially hidden, and often allocated on the basis of a single overhead rate.

v Esty, D.C. and Porter, M.E. 1998. "Industrial Ecology and Competitiveness: Strategic Implications for the Firm". Journal of Industrial Ecology, 2(1).

vi Thomas Friedman discusses this well in his book, *Hot, Flat, and Crowded* (2008).

Coda

No culture has yet solved the dilemma each has faced with the growth of the conscious mind: how to live a moral and compassionate existence when one is fully aware of the blood, the horror inherent in all life, when one finds darkness not only in one's own culture but within oneself. If there is a stage at which an individual life becomes truly adult, it must be when one grasps the irony in its unfolding and accepts responsibility for a life lived in the midst of such paradox. One must live in the middle of contradiction because if all contradiction were eliminated at once life would collapse. There are simply no answers to some of the great pressing questions. You continue to live them out, making your life a worthy expression of leaning into the light.

—Barry Lopez

I First went camping when I was 3 months old; my cozy little basket tucked under the tent flap. And so began my education in, and love of all things natural. I discovered what scientists call the hydro-riparian landscape by exploring riverbanks, especially at dusk, and I learned that if you just hunkered down and waited something extraordinary would be revealed to you: An osprey knifing through air and water to snatch a fish; a deer stepping elegantly through fireweed; an alder tree perfuming the air.

My father worked in a pulp mill – the price of living close to the wild lands he loved. We moved to the city when I was still young so I never knew, in the moment, how he squared his work in a polluting industry – something the government of the day called "the smell of money" – with his recreation, his passion. More pointedly, I will never really know what he felt when we moved to the city. Did he lose a little of himself? Or was he simply doing his best to lean into the light, to be righteous in the face of difficult choices, to make personal compromises for the sake of something bigger than himself? And what of my mother? Her roots may have been in the city, but she too loved the land, and seamlessly blended her urbanity with country life – I often fell asleep listening to Rachmaninov, one of her favorites, while the winter storms rolled across the Strait of Georgia and battered our house.

My parents adapted well to the city, and our family created a new life, a good life. I flourished in the good schools the city offered and forged career options quite distinct from those of a fishermen or mill worker. And maybe that was the point – create the opportunity for something more, something different. This is no small thing. Still, looking back on those years I think my parents' great gift to me was sustaining a connection to the land. Every summer vacation was spent camping and fishing the coastal rivers and fiords of British Columbia, and throughout the year there were day trips or "quick overnighters" to some wild place. To see salmon spawn, to count eagles, to beach comb, to, as Wallace Stegner so aptly put it, give our hearts to the mountains.

I didn't know as a young boy that the preservation of the natural world would become the unifying theme in my life, though perhaps I should have. After all, alongside the adventures, the stories, and the smells of wood smoke and canvas are lessons that accumulate and ultimately act as both an intellectual and emotional compass. The poet, Mary Oliver, calls our attention to the miracle of form and function in nature. Everything is just as it should be, hewn through the ages to meet precise needs and more – to sound a note in Leopold's orchestra of evolution. To turn away is to ignore some of the most beautiful art, the most elegant engineering, or the most affirming social behavior in the world. To turn away is also to turn away from ourselves.

Loren Eiseley would add that my early experiences in nature were about learning from creatures lacking the ability to drive a harpoon through living flesh, or to poison the air. And, as ever, he's right; nature may be red in tooth and claw, but it's an efficient economy. Nothing is done to excess, nothing is wasted, and the herd is trimmed intelligently – more intelligently than humans want to admit. And so it is that we have too many examples of Leopold's rancher who has not learned to think like a mountain and who unwittingly washes his future into the sea.

As utterly compelling as I find Oliver and Eiseley in helping to frame and interpret my experience of nature, there is something more to unfold. My experiences created the possibility of attachment, which means of course, the possibility of both joy and sorrow – joy at the singular beauty that I see in nature, and sorrow when that beauty is threatened, or indeed taken away. And the threat of sorrow is powerful; it can make you hoard your spirit. Terry Tempest Williams describes it well when she says that if we choose not to become attached to something, our heart can't be broken because we never risked giving it away. But this is no way to live, and so she exhorts us to bravely live in the world:

> But what kind of impoverishment is this to withhold emotion, to restrain our passionate nature in the face of a generous life just to appease our fears? A man or woman whose mind reins in the heart when the body sings desperately for connection can only expect more isolation and greater ecological disease. Our lack of intimacy with each other is in direct proportion to our lack of intimacy with the land. We have taken our love inside and abandoned the wild.

She is telling us to risk loving something. *This* is what my mother and father gave me. In school I would learn about community ecology, water chemistry, economics and a good deal of other, important technical knowledge that is ostensibly needed to work on behalf of nature. From my parents I learned what it is to have a visceral connection with the wild; I learned to love nature. And because of that love, I want to do what I can to protect it. I won't always be successful; my heart has been broken, the economy has grown bigger, consuming some of what I love. Still, there will be moments of grace.

As I write this, the October sun is slipping below Inverness Ridge, tendrils of light spilling over the foxglove and lavender. In the distance, marsh grasses stretch in the wind off Tomales Bay and a great egret regally surveys her domain. And there is music, the trill of a thrush that defines the rhythm and lilt of life in this corner of Point Reyes Station. I came here to write, but I have done so much more. I have opened myself to this place, and in the opening I have been seduced. Tennyson was right; I am a part of all that I have met. I now care about what happens here in a way other than the purely intellectual; I have skin in this game. I know what it is to walk through the mixed forest and fog that sheaths Tomales Point in the morning; to listen to the Pacific thundering ashore at South Beach; to watch the aeronautics of brown pelicans at Abbott's Lagoon. And because of this attachment I celebrate the wetland restoration at the head of Tomales Bay, a moment of grace against other choices that might have been made here – tract housing may be a melodramatic example, but we have seen worse done elsewhere.

So, how does this romantic meditation speak to business, society and the journey to sustainability?

I began this collection of essays with a reference to Rachel Carson's artful play on Robert Frost's poem, *The Road Not Taken*. It is worth remembering that in that poem Frost took the road less traveled by. "And that has made all the difference." It is time for business to similarly shift to a new and different road, one with which it is unfamiliar, but that can make "all the difference". As one who has worked closely with businesses all over the world, I'm sympathetic to the idea that society should reward successful initiative with profit. However, as we have seen too often, especially in the industrial age, profit-seeking activities have unhealthy side effects. And these side effects, unchecked, can eat away at the foundations of civilization. This realization led John Ruskin to suggest, as the industrial revolution was still in its nascent stages a hundred and fifty years ago, that what "seems to be wealth may in verity be only the gilded index of far-reaching ruin". An elegant wordsmith, Ruskin coined the term "illth" to describe the side effects of the economic system – poverty, pollution, despair, illness. He might well have had Charles Dickens' portrait of Coketown, the grim backdrop of his novel, *Hard Times*, in mind:

> It was a town of tall chimneys, out of which interminable serpents of smoke trailed themselves for ever and ever, and never got uncoiled. It had a black canal in it, and a river that ran purple with ill-smelling dye, and vast piles of buildings full of windows where there was rattling and trembling all day long, and where the piston of the steam-engine worked monotonously up and down, like the head of an elephant in a state of melancholy madness.

Not long after Ruskin, the American sociologist, Edward Alsworth Ross, in his masterful book, *Sin and Society*, commented on the emerging market economy of America and the role that corporations had quickly assumed in early 20th century society:

> Corporations are necessary, yet, through nobody's fault, they tend to become soulless and lawless. By all means let them reap where they have sown. But why let them declare dividends not only on their capital, but also on their power to starve out labor, to wear out litigants, to beat down small competitors, to master the market, to evade taxes, to get the free use of public property? Nothing but the curb of organized society can confine them to their own grist and keep them from grinding into dividends the stamina of children, the health of women, the lives of men, the purity of the ballot, the honor of public servants, and the supremacy of the laws.

The present book celebrates the vision of people like Leopold, Eiseley, Drucker, Cason, and others who, like Ruskin before them, saw, if not the dark side of commerce, the dangers in forgetting that the nest we too often foul is our own. It pains me to liken these good people to poor Cassandra, doomed by the god, Apollo, such that no one would believe her predictions, but that is how their story – and ours – played out over the past century. How else to explain the creation of a global economic system based on an energy source, the "Devil's tears" as John D. Rockefeller called oil, whose use slowly, and not so slowly, shreds our life support system; the failure to accelerate a response to global climate change; the failure to eliminate persistent organic pollutants and endocrine disrupters; the acceptance of dilution as a "solution" to pollution; and so on. All to support what the novelist, Henry Miller, called "lethal" comforts, conveniences and luxuries – and that's just in the West. As the economist, Jeffrey Sachs, points out, the rest of the world is rapidly joining the "economic age":

> The modern economic age is sometimes called the fossil fuel age and the 20th century could also be called the automobile

> age. But it won't work in the 21st century.
>
> There are now 900 million cars in the world, with roughly 250 million in the US – almost one car per person. That means 650 million cars for the remaining 6 billion people. China has only 50 million cars. In other words, the developing world has barely got started. Now comes the Tata Nano – a $2,500 automobile! This is a world changer. Climate change crisis, an oil crisis, a crowding and transport crisis – we are at the cusp of an unbelievable multiplication of these things.

I choose to believe that it is not too late, but the hour is long and the crises Sachs talks about constitute our greatest challenge. Through our own activities the balance in nature has shifted profoundly to our disadvantage. In October 2008, the International Union for the Conservation of Nature (IUCN) announced that at least one quarter of mammals worldwide are heading toward extinction – caused almost exclusively by human activity. In addition to the plight of mammals, the IUCN reported that reptiles, fish, and birds across the world are all in decline. Commenting on the IUCN report in *The New York Times*, Verlyn Klinkenborg drew an interesting parallel with the current convulsions in global financial markets – and the efforts to calm, if not save, them:

> What complicates matters further is a simple lesson we might also draw from the present financial crisis; everything is connected. No species goes down on its own, not without affecting the larger biological community. We emerged, as a species, from the very biodiversity we are destroying. At times it seems as though the human experiment is to see how many species we can do without. As experiments go, it is morally untenable and will end badly for us.
>
> We are watching a global, international effort to stabilize the financial markets. It will take a similar effort to begin to slow the rate at which species are declining. The bottom line is that what is good for biodiversity is good for humanity.

Is it little wonder, then, that Al Gore, in his Nobel Peace Prize lecture said the common rescue of the global environment must be the central organizing principle of the world community?

Business has a fundamental role to play in answering this call. It is the most powerful institution on the planet, and as Willis Harmon sagely noted, "the dominant institution in any society needs to take responsibility for the whole". Business has not done well when measured against this standard. David Korten, and others, argue persuasively that in the absence of government oversight, corporations are accountable only to their owners – global financial markets:

> Here we confront the implications of how the world's financial system has transformed itself. With the growth of mutual funds and retirement funds, most investment funds are now entrusted to professional investment managers whose performance may be measured by the daily results posted in the world's leading newspapers. In response to pressures for instant returns, the portfolios of these funds tend to have a high rate of turnover as fund managers speculate in the short-term price movements of stocks and other financial instruments. Focused on short-term price fluctuations, traders become increasingly detached from the real world of people, nature, and productive activity. The social and environmental consequences of their actions never register on their computer screens. Theirs is purely a world of money.

Alas, Ruskin's 19th century observation seems affirmed for the 21st century. Or is it? Could we find another path? Could we be at the edge of profound change? Does the combination of mounting evidence of ecosystem decline and the global financial crisis of 2008, the worst since the Great Depression, create the opportunity for whole system change? Could these environmental and economic convulsions push society through the doorway of what Peter Drucker called a paradigm change:

> Every few hundred years in Western history there occurs a

> sharp transformation. Within a few short decades, society -- its worldview, its basic values, its social and political structures, its arts, its key institutions -- rearranges itself. And the people born then cannot even imagine a world in which their grandparents lived and into which their own parents were born. We are currently living through such a transformation.

Can we envision, and create, a world in which business is recognized as much for its humanity, decency, maturity, understanding, and wisdom as it is for its ability to turn a profit? I think we can, but only if business comes to understand the "geography of hope", to use Stegner's phrase, in protecting (and restoring) the commons.

How will business answer this call, especially in the face of a recession where we will inevitably face the old economy versus environment debate? Among many possible responses, consider what might happen if today's business leaders, and the leaders of tomorrow, had an opportunity to experience nature – real nature, to stand beneath a mountain or beside a river with its spray in their faces as they watch it thunder into foam? Among many other benefits, one's mind clears in the wild because it is free of intrusions – telephones, e-mail, people and their noisy needs. And with a clear mind, there is the possibility of authentic, spontaneous reaction to what you see and feel – none of the self-conscious or defensive screens we too often put up at work. Imagine what nuanced and imaginative strategic plans might be hatched in the shadow of a mountain, or on the beach beside a roiling ocean? Imagine what might happen if the leaders of the businesses that presently consume nature formed an attachment to it and took the risk of loving it? Could we forge a new dialogue that links innovation, R&D, and the economy with the environment and sustainability? Could we begin to talk about how we can meet the challenges of climate change while simultaneously securing our economic future? I don't yet have an answer that satisfies me – though I am optimistic that we can, that we must, bridge the gap that has too long separated economic and environmental concerns. We can still talk about jobs, but why can't they be green jobs? We can still talk about technology, but why can't that technology be in service of solar, wind, and fuel cell power? Most importantly, we can still talk about quality of life, but why can't that quality be defined less by material consumption of goods and services and more by awareness of our individual and collective environmental footprint?

A glimpse of what I hope the future might look like can be seen in the Vehicle Design Summit (VDS), a global, open-source, collaborative effort launched by three engineering undergraduate students at the Massachusetts Institute of Technology in 2006. The VDS now has 25 member teams from universities around the world working together to build a plug-in electric hybrid within three years. Each team contributes a different set of parts or designs – all directed toward demonstrating "a 95 percent reduction in embodied energy, materials and toxicity from cradle to cradle to grave" and providing up to "200 miles per gallon energy equivalency or better." Given that transportation accounts for the majority of American oil consumption, the VDS is a fine example of an idea whose time has come. And the tagline (or manifesto) of the summit's founders says it all:

"We are the people we have been waiting for."

As Federal Governments in both America and Canada prepare to spend billions of dollars bailing out General Motors, Chrysler and Ford – the so-called "Big 3" companies that largely shunned the radical innovations in fuel efficiency and vehicle design that might have saved them – I can't help but wonder about the opportunity cost that will be charged against us and future generations. While I am not naïve to the political currents pulsing beneath the bailout conversation, are we not fundamentally propping up companies with flawed business models? What would happen if some of the money earmarked for old economy bailouts was shifted instead towards initiatives like the VDS? Or to put it more forcefully, what exciting innovations and ideas won't happen because the money that might otherwise have supported them was spent on the Big 3 and companies like them?[i]

And to assist business in its transition to a positive force for society and sustainability, the design professions should be working toward a world where every aspect of a product's lifecycle is thoughtfully considered. Where new technologies, processes, and materials are exploited to the utmost. Where costs are minimized. Where durability is as important as aesthetics. The antithesis of this, by the way, is Philip Johnson's iconic Glass House in New Canaan, Connecticut – 360 degrees of glass representing an enormous draw on energy to maintain comfort. At one time, design like this was celebrated, but in the world we need to save and restore – the world we need now – design must be informed by, and peacefully coexist with nature.

Barry Lopez, in typically lyrical fashion, argues that the central dilemma of the human experience is to live a moral and compassionate existence when one is fully aware of the blood, the horror inherent in all life, when one finds darkness not only in one's own culture but within oneself. Reading him, I am reminded of E.O. Wilson's poignant lament at the close of his extraordinary book, *The Diversity of Life:*

> If there is danger in the human trajectory, it is not so much in the survival of our own species as in the fulfillment of the ultimate irony of organic evolution: that in the instant of achieving self-understanding through the mind of man, life has doomed its most beautiful creations. And thus humanity closes the door to its past.

What will future generations write of us? What will our own children write of us? Will they marvel that with our backs to the wall we came together as never before, disenthralled ourselves from received wisdom and made our destiny a worthy expression of leaning into the light? Or will they lament our failure to do so? The hour is long and we have traveled through Frost's metaphorical yellow wood to a point where the path diverges. In one direction lies more of the same decisions and choices that will inexorably bring us to the edge of an abyss – polluting industries; inefficient use of energy and other resources; and conspicuous consumption. In the other, the one less traveled by, might lie our salvation – a new generation of businesses, and the people who run them, that has a light footprint on the Earth; a way of life defined not by consumption but by community, connection and satisfaction; an increased awareness of, and reverence for the natural world that creates the conditions for life; and a much stronger linkage of economic and cultural health with environmental health. Trend is not destiny, but it is time for us to choose our path. Let us pledge to lean into the light, to choose the path less traveled by. We might then, in a worthy echo of Frost tell our story ages and ages hence: Two roads diverged and we took the one less traveled by – and that made all the difference, that secured our future.

Notes to Coda

i By way of example, Al Gore, in his capacity as chairman of the bipartisan Alliance for Climate Protection, has called for a 10-year plan to shift the United States to "renewable energy and truly clean, carbon-free sources". To get there, Mr. Gore has proposed dramatic improvements in the national electricity grid and energy efficiency, while investing in clean solar, wind, geothermal and carbon-sequestered coal technologies. This type of plan requires massive investment, and an equally massive mindset shift – and it won't happen if we keep throwing more money at tired businesses.

Business for Social Responsibility (www.bsr.org)

A leader in corporate responsibility since 1992, Business for Social Responsibility (BSR) works with its global network of more than 250 member companies to develop sustainable business strategies and solutions through consulting, research, and cross-sector collaboration.

With six offices in Asia, Europe, and North America, BSR leverages its expertise in environment, human rights, economic development, and transparency and accountability to guide global companies toward creating a just and sustainable world.

Canadian Business for Social Responsibility (www.cbsr.ca)

Founded in 1995, CBSR is a business-led, non-profit CSR consultancy and peer-to-peer learning organization that provides its members with candid counsel and customized advisory services as they formulate powerful business decisions that improve performance and contribute to a better world.

With over 11 years of experience in corporate social responsibility, CBSR is one of the most respected organizations for CSR membership and advisory services.

Forum for the Future (www.forumforthefuture.org.uk)

The UK's leading sustainable development charity, Forum for the Future exists to accelerate the change to a sustainable way of life, taking a positive, solutions-oriented approach in everything it does. This mission is shared with partners drawn from business, finance, local government and other authorities, regional bodies, and academia.

World Business Academy (www.worldbusiess.org)

The World Business Academy is a non-profit business think tank devoted to rekindling the human spirit in business. It was founded in 1987 as a result of discussions conducted at the Stanford Research Institute (SRI) International in Menlo Park, California. These talks centered upon the role and responsibility of business in relation to the criti?cal moral, environmental and social dilemmas of the day. Led by Founder Rinaldo S. Brutoco, a small group of senior business executives and academics emerged from these meetings to create a research and education institution, the World Business Academy, to help the global business community understand and participate in the new constructive role emerging for business as the dominant institution in society.

Core areas of the Academy's research and work include sustainable business strategies, the challenge of values-driven leadership, development of the human potential at work, global reconstruction, and understanding "best practices" within new business paradigms. All of these concepts, linked together and applied, repre?sent the ongoing work of the Academy in its dialogues, research, publications, meetings, and networking. The Academy provides a collaborative network for cutting-edge business leaders, entrepre?neurs, and scholars who are aware of business' pervasive role in society. The Academy hosts world-class forums, dialogues, and retreats. It has been continuously publishing leading-edge articles for the business community for 20 years.

World Business Council for Sustainable Development (www.wbcsd.org)

The World Business Council for Sustainable Development (WBCSD) is a CEO-led, global association of some 200 companies dealing exclusively with business and sustainable development.

The Council provides a platform for companies to explore sustainable development, share knowledge, experiences and best practices, and to advocate business positions on these issues in a variety of forums, working with governments, non-governmental and intergovernmental organizations.

Members are drawn from more than 35 countries and 20 major industrial sectors. The Council also benefits from a global network of about 55 national and regional business councils and regional partners.

International Chamber of Commerce (www.icc.org)

ICC (International Chamber of Commerce) is the voice of world business championing the global economy as a force for economic growth, job creation and prosperity.

Because national economies are now so closely interwoven, government decisions have far stronger international reper-cussions than in the past.

ICC - the world's only truly global business organization responds by being more assertive in expressing business views.

ICC activities cover a broad spectrum, from arbitration and dispute resolution to making the case for open trade and the market economy system, business self-regulation, fighting corruption or combating commercial crime.

ICC has direct access to national governments all over the world through its national committees. The organization's Paris-based international secretariat feeds business views into intergovernmental organizations on issues that directly affect business operations.

International Development Program at Humber College (www.business.humber.ca)

If you want to change the world, check out the one-year post-graduate certificate in International Development offered by the business school at Toronto's Humber College.

Earth Island Journal (www.earthisland.org)

David Brower's brainchild. Enough said.

Fast Company Magazine (www.fastcompany.com)

For wild, "out-of-the-box" thinking, Fast Company can't be beat. At least 1 great idea in every issue.

Greenbiz Online Magazine (www.greenbiz.com)

A storehouse of interesting ideas from Joel Makower, one of the brightest lights in the sustainability community, to help society shift to a more sustainable trajectory - especially good recent data on eco-efficiency and performance metrics.

Innovest Strategic Value Advisors (www.innovestgroup.com)

The most elegant thinking on the relationship between environmental and financial performance, and one of the few groups that appreciates the importance of attribution.

American Planning Association (www.planning.org)

Home of the American Planning Association, an organization dedicated to providing leadership in the development of vital communities. The association's policy guide on planning for sustainability (available at www.planning.org/policyguides/sustainability) is especially useful.

Small Potatoes Urban Delivery (www.small-potatoes.com)

David Van Seters, a friend, colleague and inspiration, has built Canada's largest home delivery organic grocery company as a model of sustainability. Watch this energetic company and learn what it means to be sustainable...and successful.

World Resources Institute (www.wri.org)

Home of Robert Repetto, architect of some of the most cogent economic studies on sustainability available anywhere. His recent work, with Duncan Austin, on disclosure of environmental risks (or lack thereof) in the U.S. pulp and paper industry is especially good reading.

Bibliography

Abbott, R.M. 2008. *Uncommon Cents: Thoreau and the Nature of Business*. Sheffield, VT: Green Frigate Books.

Bansal, P. 2005. "Evolving Sustainably: A Longitudinal Study of Corporate Sustainable Development", *Strategic Management Journal*, 26: 197-218.

Barnes, p. 2006. *Capitalism 3.0: a guide to reclaiming the commons*. San Francisco: berrett-koehler publishers, inc.

Benyus, J. 1997. *Biomimicry: Innovation Inspired by Nature.* New York: Quill.

Brower, D. and Chapple, S. 1996. *Let the Mountains talk, Let the Rivers Run: A Call to Those Who Would Save the Earth.* San Francisco: HarperSanFrancisco.

Cairncross, F. 1991. *Costing the Earth*. Boston: Harvard Business School Press.

Carson, R. 1962. *Silent Spring.* Greenwich: Fawcett Publications, Inc.

Chouinard, Y. 2005. *Let my people go surfing.* New York: The Penguin Press.

Commoner, B. 1971. *The Closing Circle: Nature, Man & Technology.* New york: bantam books.

Cosgrove, D. and Daniels, S. (eds.) 1988. *Iconography of Landscape.* Cambridge: Cambridge University Press.

Colby, M. 1990. *Environmental Management in Development: The Evolution of Paradigms*. New York: World Bank Discussion Paper (No.80).

Daily, G. C. (ed.) 1997. *Nature's Services: Societal Dependence on Natural Ecosystems*. Washington, D.C.: Island Press.

Daly, H.E. 1996. *Beyond Growth: The Economics of Sustainable Development.* Boston: Beacon Press.

Daly, H. E. and Townsend, K.N. (eds.) 1996. *Valuing the Earth: Economics, Ecology, Ethics.* Cambridge, MA: The MIT Press.

Daly, H.E. and Cobb, J.B. Jr. 1994. *For The Common Good: Redirecting the Economy Toward Community, The Environment, and a Sustainable Future,* 2nd ed. Boston: Beacon Press.

Daly, H.E. (ed.) 1973. *Toward a Steady-State Economy.* San Francisco: W.H. Freeman and Company.

Eblen, R.A. and Eblen, W.R. 1994. *The Encyclopedia of the Environment*. Boston: Houghton Mifflin Company.

Eckbo, G. 1950. *Landscape for Living*. New York: F.W. Dodge Corporation.

Eiseley, I. 1969. *The Unexpected Universe*: San Diego: Harcourt Brace Jovanovich.

Ibid. 1957. *The Immense Journey: An Imaginative Naturalist Explores the Mysteries of Man and Nature*. New York: Vintage Books, Random House.

Elkington, J. 1997. *Cannibals with Forks: The Triple Bottom Line of 21st Century Business*. Oxford: Capstone Publishing Limited.

Elkington, J. 1994. "Towards the Sustainable Corporation: Win-Win-Win Business Strategies for Sustainable Development", *California Management Review*, 36(2): 90-100.

Field, B.C. and Olewiler, N.D. 1995. *Environmental Economics*. Toronto: McGraw-Hill Ryerson Limited.

France, R. 2006. *Introduction to Watershed Development: Understanding and Managing the Impacts of Sprawl*. Lanham, Maryland: Rowman & Littlefield Publishers, Inc.

Galbraith, J.K. 1996. *The Good Society: the Humane Agenda*. Boston: Houghton Mifflin company.

Ibid. 1958. *The Affluent Society*. Boston: Houghton Mifflin company.

Gide, A. 1932. Preface. *In Night Flight*, by A. de Saint-Exupery, pp. v-xi. New York: Century Co.

Glacken, C. 1967. *Traces on the Rhodian Shore: Nature and Culture in Western Thought from Ancient Times to the End of the Eighteenth Century*. Berkeley: University of California Press.

Gore, A. 2007. *Our Purpose: The Nobel Peace Prize Lecture*. New York: Rodale, Inc.

Gray, P.E. 1989. "The Paradox of Technological Development" In J.H. Ausubel and H.E. Sladovich, eds., *Technology and Environment*. Washington, D.C.: National Academy Press.

Grescoe, T. 2008. "Finny Finis?", *The Globe and Mail*, Saturday, July 26, 2008, pp. D8-9.

Haddon, W. 1970. "On the Escape of Tigers: An Ecologic Note." *Technology Review* 6: 45-48.

Hart, S.L. 1997. "Beyond Greening: Strategies for a Sustainable World" *Harvard Business Review*, January-February.

Hart, S.L. and Milstein, M.B. 1999. "Global Sustainability and the Creative Destruction of Industries", *Sloan Management Review*, 41: 23-34.

Hawken, P. 1994. *The Ecology of Commerce: A Declaration of Sustainability*. New York: HarperBusiness.

Hawken, P. et al. 1999. *Natural capitalism: Creating the Next Industrial Revolution*. Boston: Little, Brown.

Hemingway, E. 1926. *The Sun Also Rises*. New York: Scribner.

Henderson, H. 1968. "Should Business Tackle Society's Problems?", Harvard Business Review, 46: 77-85.

Hess, D. et al. 2002. "The Next Wave of Corporate Community Involvement: Corporate Social Initiatives", *California Management Review*, 44: 110-125.

Hillman, A.J. and Keim, G.D. 2001. "Shareholder Value, Stakeholder Management, and Social Issues: What's the Bottom Line?", *Strategic Management Journal*, 22: 125-139.

Holling, C.S. 1998. "The Renewal, Growth, Birth and Death of Ecological Communities" *Whole Earth*, Summer.

Humboldt, A. Von. 1844. *Cosmos, vol. 1 and 2*. New York: Harper and Brothers.

Ikenberry, J.G. 1993. "The Political Origins of Bretton Woods" In M.D. Bordo and B. Eichengreen, eds., *A Retrospective on the Bretton Woods System: Lessons for International Monetary Reform*. Chicago: University of Chicago Press.

IUCN - The World Conservation Union. 1991. *Caring for the Earth: A Strategy for Sustainable Living*. Switzerland: Earth Scan Publishing.

Jackson, I.A. and Nelson, J. 2004. *Profits with Principles: Seven Strategies for Delivering Value with Values*. New York: CurrencyDoubleday.

Jacobs, J. 2000. *The Nature of Economies*. Toronto: Random House Canada.

Ibid. 1992. *The Death and Life of Great American Cities*. New york: vintage books.

Jensen, J. 1930. "Natural Parks and Gardens", *Saturday Evening Post*, March 8.

Korhonen, J. 2002. "The Dominant Economics Paradigm and Corporate Social Responsibility", *Corporate Social Responsibility and Environmental Management*, 9: 67-80.

Kotter, J. and Rathgeber, H. 2005. *Our Iceberg is Melting: Changing and Succeeding Under Any Conditions*. New York: St. Martins Press.

Krueger, R.R. and Mitchell, B., eds. 1976. *Managing Canada's Renewable Resources*. Toronto: Methuen.

Lane, P. 2004. *There is a Season: A Memoir.* Toronto: McClelland and Stewart Ltd.?

Lerner, S. 1998. *Eco-Pioneers: Practical Visionaries Solving Today's Environmental Problems*. Cambridge, MA: The MIT Press.

Leopold, A. 1949. *A Sound County Almanac and Sketches Here and There*. New York: Oxford University Press.

Linden, E. 2002. *The Future in Plain Sight: The Rise of the "True Believers" and Other Clues to the Coming Instability*. New York: Plume Printing.

Lopez, B. 1986. *Arctic Dreams: Imagination and Desire in a Northern Landscape*. New York: Charles Scribner's Sons.

Lowenthal, D. 1967. *Geography, Experience and Imagination: Towards a Geographical Epistemology*. In Cultural Geograpy: Selected Readings, ed. F.E. Dohrs and L.E. Sommers, pp. 71-91. New York: Thomas Y. Crowell.

Ibid. 1985. *The Past is a Foreign Country*. Cambridge: Cambridge University Press.

Macy, J. and Brown, M.Y. 1998. *Coming Back to Life: Practices to Reconnect Our Lives, Our World*. Gabriola Island: New Society Publishers.

Martin, R. 2002. "The Virtue Matrix", *Harvard Business Review*, 80: 68-76.

McDonough, W. and Braungart, M. 2002. *Cradle to Cradle: Remaking the Way We Make Things*. New York: North Point Press.

McGuire, J.W. and Parrish, J.B. 1971. "Status Report on a Profound Revolution", *California Management Review*, 13: 79-86.

Meadows, D.H. et al. 1972. The Limits to Growth. London: Earth Island.

Miller, H. 1945. The air-conditioned nightmare. New york: new directions books.

Nash, R.F. 1981. *Wilderness and the American Mind, 3rd ed.* New Haven and London: Yale University Press.

Nestruck, J.K. 2008. "A refreshing window into a foreign time", *The Globe and Mail*, Monday, June 30, 2008, p. R7.

Nicolis, G. and Prigogine, I. 1989. *Exploring Complexity*. New York: W.H. Freeman.

Nikiforuk, A. 2008. "Oil Disquiet on the Western front?", *The Globe and Mail*, Saturday, June 28, 2008, p. D15.

Nordhause, T. and Schellenberger, M. 2007. *Breakthrough: From the Death of Environmentalism to the Politics of Possibility*. Boston: Houghton-Mifflin Co.

Norton, B.G. and Toman, M.A. 1997. "Sustainability: Ecological and Economic Perspectives", *Land Economics*, 73: 553-569.

Peat Marwick Stevenson & Kellog. 1993. *1993 Environmental Scan: Evaluating Our Progress Toward Sustainable Development*. Prepared for the Canadian Council of Ministers of the Environment, CCME-SPC-74E.

Porter, M.E. and Kramer, M.R. 2006. "Strategy & Society: The Link Between Competitive Advantage and Corporate Social Responsibility", *Harvard Business Review*, December, pp. 76-92.

Porritt, J. 2005. *Capitalism as if the World Mattered*. London: Earthscan.

Prakash, A. 2001. "Why Do Firms Adopt 'Beyond-Compliance' Environmental Policies?", *Business Strategy and the Environment*, 10: 286-299.

Quammen, D. "An Endangered Idea". *National Geographic*, October 2006, 62-67.

Roman, R.M. et al. 1999. "The Relationship Between Social and Financial Performance", *Business & Society*, 38: 109-126.

Ross, E.A. 1907. *Sin and Society*. Boston: Houghton Mifflin Company.

Ross, W.M. 1973. *Oil Pollution as an International Problem: A Study of Puget Sound and the Strait of Georgia*. Western Geographcal Series, Volume 6. Victoria: University of Victoria.

Russo, M.V. 2003. "The Emergence of Sustainable Industries: Building on Natural Capital", *Strategic Management Journal*, 24: 317-331.

Saint-Exupery, A. de. 1932. *Night Flight*. New York: Century Co.

Ibid. 1939. *Wind, Sand and Stars*. New York: Reynal & Hitchcock.

Ibid. 1986. *Wartime Writings 1939-1944*. San Diego: Harcourt Brace Jovanovich.

Sauer, C.O. 1965. *The Morphology of Landscape*. In Land and Life, ed. J. Leighly, pp. 315-50. Berkeley: University of California Press.

Schama, S. 1995. *Landscape and Memory*. New York: Knopf.

Snyder, G. 1974. Turtle Island. New York: New Directions Books.

Solnit, R. 2004. *Hope in the Dark: Untold Histories, Wild Possibilities*. Toronto: Penguin Group.

Soros, G. 2008. "The Perilous Price of Oil", *The New York Review of Books*, September 25, 2008, pp36-38.

Steinbeck, J. 1939. *The Grapes of Wrath*. New York: Viking.

Thayer, R.L. 1994. *Gray World, Green Heart: Technology, Nature, and the Sustainable Landscape*. New York:John Wiley & Sons, Inc.

Thomas, W.L. ed. 1956. *Man's Role in Changing the Face of the Earth*. Chicago: University of Chicago Press.

Turner, F.W. 1983. *Beyond Geography: The Western Spirit Against the Wilderness.* New Brunswick, N.J.: Rutgers University Press.

Union of Concerned Scientists. 1993. *World Scientists' Warning to Humanity*. Washington, D.C.

Von Weizsacker, E. et al. 1997. *Factor Four: Doubling Wealth, Halving Resource Use*. London: Earthscan Publications.

Wackernagel, M. and Rees, W. 1995. *Our Ecological Footprint: Reducing Human Impact on the Earth*. Gabriola Island, B.C.: New Society Publishers.

Wiggins, R.R. and Ruefli, T.W. 2005. "Schumpeter's Ghost: Is Hypercompetition Making the Best of Times Shorter?", *Strategic Management Journal*, 26: 887-911.

Wilson, A. 1991. *The Culture of Nature: North American Landscape from Disney to the Exxon Valdez*. Toronto: Between the Lines.

Worster, D. 1977. *Nature's Economy: A History of Ecological Ideas*. Cambridge: Cambridge University Press.

Wright, J.K. 1966. *Terrae Incognitae: The Place of the Imagination in Geography.* In Human Nature in Geography, ed. J.K. Wright, pp. 68-88. Cambridge, MA: Harvard University Press.

Wright, R. 2004. *A Short History of Progress*. Toronto: House of Anansi Press Inc.

Youngquist, W. GeoDestinies: The Inevitable Control of Earth Resources Over Nations and Individuals. New York: National Book Company, 1977.

Zadek, S. et al. (eds.) 1997. *Building Corporate Accountability: Emerging Practices in Social and Ethical Accounting, Auditing and Reporting*. London: Earthscan Publications Ltd.

Index

About the Author

Rob Abbott is one of Canada's leading sustainability strategists. Over the past twenty years he has helped businesses all over the world discover wealth-creating opportunities through a deeper integration of sustainability with organizational and competitive strategy. He is not only a highly sought after speaker on this topic, but also a passionate mentor and coach for students and social entrepreneurs wishing to explore the business value of sustainability. Rob's clients include leading TSX, NYSE, and Fortune/S&P 500 firms, as well as new venture enterprises. A core focus of his current work is helping businesses worldwide embrace the audacious thinking necessary to transition to a less carbon intensive economy – at a time when global demand for energy is rising sharply.

A Certified Management Consultant, Rob frames corporate responsibility and sustainability in a strategic business context that guides organizations to the creation and implementation of programs that deliver both shareholder and stakeholder value, and create or burnish a brand reputation. He is particularly interested in helping organizations push past organizational effectiveness and embrace true organizational transformation through sustainability. Rob completed undergraduate work in geography at the University of Victoria, and Masters Degrees in geography and environmental studies at the University of Toronto, before undertaking Doctoral studies in resource and environmental management at Simon Fraser University. He is the author of *Uncommon Cents: Thoreau and the Nature of Business* (2008), the strategy columnist for *Green Business Magazine*, and a frequent commentator on sustainability and business strategy in regional and national magazines and newspapers in Canada.

Scriptorium/Palimpsest Press

In medieval times, monk scholars would gather in the scriptorium and reuse valuable sheets of vellum parchment that had once contained previous words and images. In a similar spirit of conservation, Scriptorium/Palimpsest Press is devoted to collecting and republishing earlier palimpsest tracings.